DEMCO

Lee Quinby

Millennial
seduction

A Skeptic Confronts Apocalyptic Culture

CORNELL UNIVERSITY PRESS   Ithaca & London

First published 1999 by Cornell University Press.

Library of Congress Cataloging-in-Publication Data
Quinby. Lee, b. 1946
    Millennial seduction : a skeptic confronts apocalyptic culture /
    by Lee Quinby.
        p.   cm.
    Includes bibliographical references and index.
    ISBN 0-8014-3592-7 (cloth : alk. paper)
    ISBN 0-8014-8601-7 (paperback)
    1. Skepticism.   2. Millennium.   3. End of the world.   I. Title.
    BL2747.Q56   1999
    306—dc21   98-46230
Printed in the United States of America.

For three chapters, I have drawn on the following earlier essays:

" 'Sex Respect': Thoreau, the Religious Right, and the Problem of Chastity," *Prose Studies* (1994): 20–38.

"Coercive Purity: The Dangerous Promise of Apocalyptic Masculinity." In *The Year 2000*, edited by Charles Strozier and Michael Flynn, pp. 154–65. New York: New York University Press, 1997.

"Technoppression and the Intricacies of Cyborg Flesh," *Constellations* (1997): 229–47

Cloth printing   10   9   8   7   6   5   4   3   2   1
Paperback printing   10   9   8   7   6   5   4   3   2   1

CONTENTS

For my parents, Miriam and Thomas Quinby

ACKNOWLEDGMENTS

It is one of the pleasures of book writing to be able, in this public way, to thank those who have helped make the process both possible
and meaningful. I feel fortunate to belong to an intellectual community
that stretches between Hobart and William Smith Colleges, in Geneva,
New York, where I teach, and New York City, where I live when I am not
teaching. I am particularly grateful to members of reading groups in
each place. In Geneva, the Not Piss Poor Academy has been meeting for
several years now to discuss works in progress. Thanks to Betty Bayer,
Claudette Columbus, Jodi Dean, Manisha Desai, Maureen Flynn, Susan
Henking, A'Lelia Henry, and Christina Sharpe for reading two chapters
at early stages and nudging me toward more incisive prose and ways to
develop my thinking. My New York reading group has been a mainstay
of my thinking since 1991. Thanks to the "original" members, Kate
Mehuron, Margaret Walker, Mary Katherine Wainwright, and Patricia
Mann, and to the newer members, Donald Mengay, Elayne Rapping, and
Frances Bartkowski.

Hobart and William Smith Colleges has been a terrific place to work
while writing this book. Two research grants helped enormously, one
making it possible for me to travel to Patmos and the other to Washington, D.C. The interest and impressive intelligence of a number of students
from various classes at Hobart and William Smith have allowed me to
think out loud and get feedback on many of the topics in this book; for
this I am especially grateful to Marin Lorenson, Alison Sherrick, Megan
Myers-Hayes, Samantha Marrin, Amber Hoover, and Jody Gould. I would

like to thank student assistants Laurel Allen, Juliet Evans, Michelle Lo-
heac, and Rene de Gironemo who have gathered information over the
years. The innovative curriculum of the colleges has supported my scholarly efforts as well. I have been able to concentrate on issues of apocalypse and millennium by offering first-year and senior seminars with
those titles. The interdisciplinary emphasis of the curriculum enabled
me to plan and co-teach a course with my colleague Jodi Dean from the
Political Science Department. Our bidisciplinary course, "Technologies
of Truth: Aliens and Cyborgs," has been one of the high points of my
teaching career. Jodi has been especially important to this book in several ways. She read and commented on almost every chapter, some of
them twice. I am also indebted to her for an invitation to write an essay
that eventually became the final chapter of the book. She will understand the inside joke when I say that as a teacher and friend she has been
a "real McCoy."

Because my preoccupation with issues of apocalypse has lasted
throughout the 1990s, I have engaged many friends and colleagues in
what I like to think of as a sustained conversation on the Millennium.
Tom Hayes has been vital to my thinking. Colleagues at the University of
Athens who have remained friends long past my Fulbright stay have illuminated this and many other topics; my special thanks to Bessie Dendrinos, Eleni Haviara-Kehaidou, and John Chioles. Adrienne Leban added
to my collection of Promise Keepers materials and offered important
suggestions on an earlier draft. Wendy Fairey provided excellent company and a wicked wit. Anna Marie Smith listened to me agonize over titles for months and then solved the problem by deftly summing up my
focus as millennial seduction.

Having the opportunity to give some of the early drafts of these
chapters as presentations has proved invaluable. I am grateful to Vincent
Colapietro and John Stuhr at Penn State University for including me in
their philosophy conference on Foucault; to Nancy K. Miller and Louis
Menand for inviting me to the Twentieth Century Seminar at the CUNY
Graduate Center; to Robert Jay Lifton, Michael Flynn, and Charles
Strozier at the John Jay Center on Violence and Survival; to John
McGowan for organizing an MLA panel on "Theoretical Controversy";

and to Tom Tobin, Josh Slifkin, and Jean Schulte at Duquesne University for their wonderful Graduate Student Conference on "Order and Disorder." Thanks to Malini Johar Schueller and Tina Pippin for providing the opportunity to write essays that have been revised for this book. A special thanks goes to Richard Landes, Director of the Center for Millennial Studies at Boston University, for his energy in establishing archives and organizing conferences on the history and current expression of apocalypticism.

Alison Shonkwiler has been a superb editor from start to finish. I am indebted to Stephen O'Leary for his constructive reading of the manuscript, particularly his suggestion for reorganization, and to Charles Strozier for his support and recommendations for improvement.

I also want to thank my sons and daughters-in-law, Michael and Elana Dougatz Miller and Paul Miller and Terry Freeman, for their support of my work. They make it worth doing.

Finally and most of all, I am happy to dedicate this book to my parents. Miriam and Thomas Quinby are remarkable in many ways. After nearly sixty years of marriage, during which they raised six children and bravely confronted almost every possible family crisis that can occur, they remain the most affectionate couple I know. They are both sharply intelligent and uncommonly considerate of others. Until writing this book, I had never thought of them as skeptics, in part because their spiritual lives are so different from mine. But I have had to rethink a lot of things in the process of writing this book and have come to appreciate their everyday generosities and rare ability to confront myriad difficulties with exceptional grace. In this regard, I would say that they are skeptics, Southern style.

LEE QUINBY

Geneva, New York

INTRODUCTION
THRESHOLD OF REVELATION

Our daily lives, from the way we perceive the weather to how we experience our bodies and conjure the future, have been ingrained with the textures of apocalyptic belief. A case in point: January 1998 brought severe ice storms to the upstate region of New York. Heavy ice downed electricity lines and made roadways impassable. Life was surely difficult. But was this divine action? At least one member of the stricken area thought so. Consequently, a CNN reporter quoted this person's observation without reflection: "It's preparation for Armageddon."

If this were an isolated incident, it wouldn't be worth pointing to it. Such blurring of religious and secular apocalypticism, however, is hardly isolated, even in regard to the weather. The warming trend known as El Niño has been depicted in largely apocalyptic terms, from its name meaning "little Christ child" to recurrent evocations of its mysterious yet all-encompassing destructiveness. Doomsdayers abound, pointing to famines in Africa, the spread of AIDS, techniques of cloning, urban decay, and dying fish in Maryland waters as signs of the End. Threats of worldwide computer calamity from the millennium bug range from frozen ATMs to jammed elevators to misfiring missiles.[1] Throughout the final decade of the twentieth century, Saddam Hussein has been drawn as, if not *the* Anti-Christ, one of his forerunners. Nostradamians insist that our time is up.

Millennial hope is equally widespread and eclectic. Not only have apparitions of the Virgin Mary multiplied, but also scientific pantheism insists that Gaia will convert the disharmonious energy plaguing earth and its inhabitants into a grand equilibrium. What has been dubbed the New Spirituality, a blend of multiculturalism and spiritual progress, has been spurred on variously by end-of-the-millennium jitters, popular astrology's attention to the dawning Age of Aquarius, and renewed efforts of groups like the Campus Crusaders. Hundreds of thousands of men have twice gathered in Washington, D.C., to commit themselves to new manhood for the New Era. In a time when Jesus is online, more than 80 percent of Americans believe in heaven, angel icons are propagating in department stores, and guardian angel stories have become prime-time media coverage. On top of everything, genetic research promises to deliver the "perfect baby."[2]

Americans have been taught to reside in apocalyptic terror and count on millennial perfection. For a substantial number, this is an intense Bible-based fundamentalism. For a larger majority, these fears and hopes are far more nebulous, a loose blend of religious symbols and secular expression. In the United States, this imprecise yet overpowering belief system is a way of life. But what if we were taught to live skeptically? What benefits might we experience from so seismic a shift? What personal and societal changes would be necessary to make skepticism as a way of life possible? And what new meanings would skepticism have in the contemporary United States, a culture dramatically different from the ancient Greek society from which skepticism emerged as a philosophical school?

This book was written with those questions and two interrelated aims in mind. My first aim is to forge a skeptical perspective specifically in regard to apocalyptic and millennialist belief. This means examining some of the primary vehicles for each in the United States, particularly education, sexuality, and technology. My second goal is to seek out ways of thinking and living that endorse hope, aspiration, and transformation without capitulating to apocalyptic fever and millennial mania.

Promoting ways of thinking and living unhampered by fear of earth-shattering catastrophe and extricated from the kindred conviction that a perfect world is on the horizon is admittedly an uphill task. Endism has long run deep in the United States, ranging from a literal acceptance of the divine apocalypse predicted in the Book of Revelation to a more nebulous sense of impending doom, whether from asteroids, viruses, or technology.³ Believing that the end of the world looms means living in the shadow of fear. Some believers report suffering intensely whereas others disclose a more general anxiety or routine agitation.

What makes living with apocalyptic belief tolerable for so many is its accompanying millennial dream, the current of hope that promises the fullness of Truth unveiled and visions of perfection for the elect. The elect are the chosen ones, whether they be divinely ordained, technologically proficient, or just plain lucky, the ones tapped to survive destruction and reign supreme in the millennium. Not that such hope is the antidote to fear—at least not the kind that is framed in apocalyptic zeal. Apocalyptic fear and millennialist hope fit hand in glove, with the glove of augmented desire needing the hand of inordinate fear to fill out its shape. I call this sense of millennial hope *electism*, not only to highlight its relation to endism, but also to make clear the inherent divisiveness of apocalypse. Even when electism takes a benign, generous and nebulous form, division and hierarchy prevail. For example, although the spiritual progress of New Age belief is supposed to envelop the whole world and for some the universe, the concept of the elect remains. It is simply extended to all in a promised transformation toward higher consciousness; the partition between the chosen and the doomed becomes temporal, dividing between the former and new ages.⁴ More often, however, electism is cast overtly in oppositional terms in keeping with the fierce battle between the forces of good and evil envisioned in Revelation.

The rub, of course, is that it is impossible to disprove apocalyptic prophecy once and for all. But it can't be proven either; even the most ardent believers concede that faith is necessary. In the meantime, it should be possible to shift focus to the historical record of apocalyptic and millennialist belief. First, the end of the world has not arrived as predicted. This seems obvious, but given the recurrent insistence that the end is near, it needs to be stated bluntly. The failure rate of this prediction over the course of 2000 years is pretty astounding. If more than two millennia have passed since apocalyptic writings emerged in Jewish and then Christian society, there is no good evidence to accept them as applicable to the present. Even though natural calamities and technological disasters do happen, there is no historical or scientific evidence to link such occurrences to supernatural agency. And although there are well-known stories that tell of world-ending calamities—the biblical flood, for example—such disasters are more likely to be exaggerations of earthquakes, volcanoes, and mudslides that may have destroyed whole societies, but not the earth. Whatever the cause of the flood that Noah survived, it is obviously clear that—despite numerous predictions—world-destructive disasters, such as earthquakes, floods, asteroids, and so on, have not happened. So my first point is what *hasn't* happened.

My second point is what *has* happened as a result of the rise and spread of apocalypticism and millennialism as *systems of belief*. Apocalypticism claims that a supernatural or exceedingly powerful force, like nuclear disaster, for example, will bring world destruction, but that an elect number will be granted a new, transformed earth. This powerful conviction that time and the world as we know it are ending has brought both terror and fervor to multitudes over the centuries. As many scholars have pointed out, such a belief is far more likely to accompany poverty and persecution than privilege. Heartfelt expression for suffering to come to an end has a history of spurring struggle. This struggle includes holy wars against earthly forces believed to be under the sway of Satan as well as personal vendettas against forces of technology, by the unabomber, for example.

Like apocalyptic endism, millennialist electism also stems most notably from the Book of Revelation, specifically Chapter 20, Verse 4,* which proclaims that the martyred faithful will be returned to enjoy a thousand-year reign with the son of God while Satan is bound away in a lake of fire. From the Crusades to the colonization of the Americas to the Cold War, millennialism has spurred desire to be one of the elect, desire bolstered by apocalyptic demands to fight against forces of evil. The sense of being chosen to survive the days of doom easily conflates with believing one has been called to enact them, thereby bringing about the New Era. The twentieth century alone provides ample evidence of this, including one of its most atrocious brands of apocalyptic millennialism,

* All Bible references for this book are from the Authorized (King James) Version.

the Third Reich, as well as its current white-supremacist and militia off-shoots.

Evoking Nazism is not meant to be alarmist. While I do want to insist that millennialist belief has been a powerful moving force for social domination, I also want to acknowledge, as Stephen Jay Gould has put it, that there probably will be more party than terror this time around.[5] Nevertheless, it is important not to dismiss the detrimental effects of apocalypticism and millennialism, not only in U.S. culture, which is the focus of this book, but also around the world.[6] What this book stresses is that apocalyptic and millennialist principles and practices interfere with the goals of democratic societies.

My view runs contrary to scholars who regard apocalyptic zeal as necessary to democratic social transformation, as indeed essential to the establishment of the United States as a democracy and to the achievements of the civil rights movement in the sixties and of second-wave feminism.[7] This stance emerged out of Norman Cohn's highly influential work *The Pursuit of the Millennium,* which details a number of links between apocalyptic belief and egalitarian movements.[8] But it is a reductive reading of Cohn's complex account, which situates what he calls "revolutionary millenarianism" in relation to other social movements in Europe between the eleventh and seventeenth centuries. He points out that both peasant revolts and urban insurrections were "very common and moreover often successful," contrasting them to apocalyptic groups which came together from an "unorganized, atomized population, rural or urban or both." Banding together around a charismatic prophet, often an intellectual, including former priests, rather than one of the poor, the millenarian groups typically had leaders who were obsessed with the end-time. Unlike the populist social movements, these fringe groups embodied a kind of radical desperation. Stances linking apocalypse to democracy tend to overlook the ways in which strident apocalyptic conviction propels such marginalized groups toward martyrdom or genocidal massacre because of their willingness to defy their enemies.[9] When these designated enemies are as powerful as the U.S. government, incidents like Waco can occur. Similarly, many other groups run the danger of confusing unconditional defiance with radical social change in the name of democratic practice.

Millennialist groups with less focus on apocalyptic catastrophe have fared better. In the United States, there have been numerous efforts to establish utopian societies, such as in Harmony, Pennsylvania. Though some of these social efforts have lasted for many decades, they often experience legal and social clashes resulting from their millennialist desires for total emancipation from societal law and norm. One contribution these groups make to skeptical thinking is the way they highlight social and legal constraint on individual freedom. Nevertheless, many of them, bent on achieving their heaven on earth, enforce rigid constraints of their own. That makes visible the significant differences between being inspired toward millennial community and achieving democratic society.

Although many of the leaders of the American Revolution may have been millennialist in their outlook, it does not follow that such belief is the main ingredient of a democratic system. Indeed, I am arguing that many of the obstacles U.S. democracy has faced and currently confronts are rooted in its millennialism. At the same time, I am arguing that the strengths of U.S. democracy stem from the skepticism that is also present in the founding documents, built into the Constitution's Bill of Rights, especially the separation of church and state, its system of checks and balances, and provisions for amendment. Without a constructive skepticism of this sort, millennialist fatalism would be far more likely to breed indifference about the here and now or even a willingness to be an agent of apocalyptic terrorism than to strengthen democratic participation. The civil rights movement stands in contrast to either of those paths. It is undeniable that the movement was propelled by a faith-based belief in being chosen by God to pursue freedom. Rather than waiting for a heavenly reward, however, this movement employed skepticism to spur its democratic activism for change, not in the hereafter, but here and now. A wonderful example is Martin Luther King's "Letter from a Birmingham Jail." Although it gathers rhetorical force through appeals to a morality in accord with God's higher law, his careful analysis of what constitutes a just law versus an unjust one is a skeptic's adroit justification for why and how undemocratic process should be altered. In short, I argue that endism and electism, whether religious or secular, undermine the principles and practices of democracy that are bolstered by skepticism.

Both apocalyptic consternation and millennialist confidence are palpably rising as we approach the opening decade of a third millennium. At the very least, we face years of intense media hype. With democratic process in mind, party rather than terror is not exactly a salve. Experience has shown that celebration and terrorism don't emerge independently of one another, as the bombing at the 1996 Atlanta Olympics illustrates. Even more frightening, one act of terrorism can decimate many lives, as the bombings of the Federal Building in Oklahoma and the National Trade Center in New York City make clear. Therefore we may be concerned about the consumerism heralding the millennium as the party to end all parties. It is hardly a boon to democratic practice. In fact, in order to have mega-celebrations for the year 2000, huge policing efforts are being put in place as a way of preventing the kind of crowd bombing that occurred in Atlanta. At the worst, Armageddon-inspired goals, whether religious or secular, will erupt in rampant violence and warfare. Either way, without concerted effort to alter public opinion, it is unlikely that apocalypticism will suddenly disappear when the third millennium begins. One doesn't have to be a prophet to say that the opening years of the twenty-first century/third millennium will bear the mark of the closing years of the twentieth century/second millennium.

On a more positive side, the significance we accord to the beginning of a new millennium also provides possibilities for reflection. It is an opportunity for public education, a way to make visible the effects of apocalyptic systems of belief on societies. In endorsing a present-day skeptical stance, then, I am not arguing for a return to the skepticism of ancient philosophy, outlined as the Skeptic Way by Sextus Empiricus. My view is hardly a retreat to a Golden Age—there never was one for women anyway and I disagree outright with the social and legal conformity upheld in that doctrine. It is, rather, an attempt to figure out how to live both skeptically and meaningfully in an era marked by the inception of a new millennium and to question inherited tenets of social custom, religion, and law, especially to the extent that they have derived from apocalyptic belief. That is an intimidating order, given the pervasiveness of apocalypticism and millennialism as a palpable presence in the United States. But if democracy is a goal, it is worth the effort. The ongoing questioning that is characteristic of skepticism might not bring the tranquility of mind that Sextus Empiricus assumed it would, but if it shields against overwhelming anxieties, hatred, questionable hopes, and dogmatic zeal, it has discernible value.

The way of thinking and living that I am advocating is in keeping with what John Rajchman has said about the skepticism advanced by Michel Foucault. Rather than asking "skeptical questions about 'experience in general,'" Rajchman writes, Foucault "asks skeptical questions about the very idea of subsuming our sciences, rationalities, subjectivities, languages, or techniques of rule, under a single philosophical category such as 'experience in general.'"[10] As a mode of inquiry and a way of living, this form of skepticism encourages analysis of how truths are culturally established and embodied as experience. Millennial skepticism specifically questions truth claims that are authorized through faith alone, whether its source of authority derives from the divine, the natural and social sciences and the humanities, or the legal system. It also confronts the ways in which the empirical claims of these various sources of authority are framed, looking to their historical constitution to track the relations of power and the cultural conditions that built such edifices of knowledge.

This questioning of "experience in general" has long been integral to feminist modes of analysis. Therefore my advocacy of millennial skepticism draws extensively from feminist challenges to masculinist claims for universal experience. It follows that skeptical questioning needs to be applied to both Foucauldian and feminist thought as well. Doing so exposes the ways in which both of these modes of inquiry have at various times appealed to apocalyptic urgencies and millennialist dreams. I am arguing that such appeals thwart the democratic orientation of these otherwise skeptical modes of inquiry. The strength of feminist and Foucauldian analysis lies in their situated, systematic doubt about masculinist thought and practice, which for centuries has bolstered its power and justified its gender, sex, and race hierarchies by playing on apocalyptic fear and deferring equality and justice to some future moment. Millennial skepticism, which at various times I refer to as "skeptical revelation," "genealogical skepticism," and "Jezebelian skepticism," depending on a particular emphasis, is a deliberate and deliberative means to challenge the reign of masculinist thought and the truth of apocalypse.

I frequently draw on works of literature as a way of confronting one truth with another. My rationale is not that literature possesses universal or timeless truth, but that as a discourse it has been accorded a certain truth status in our society, one that often conflicts with monolithic truth claims. To the extent that literature encourages multiple and even conflicting meanings, it encourages millennial skepticism. In other words, my purpose is not to derive from literature a single voice that imposes harmony on the conflicting strands. It is, rather, to highlight the conflict and search for a way to tell the truth as best I can and to tell what I regard as the best truth—skeptical truth. From this point of view, literature is a mode of knowledge that intertwines not only with our personal bodies and histories as readers but also with our civic bodies and national histories. For similar reasons, I also draw on popular culture, especially film and television, because both are forms of expression that have their own claims to truth in our day. Both have what Roland Barthes called a "reality effect," in many cases far stronger than literature these days, blending as they do with news reporting and the evidence of images. All three forms of expression, literature, film, and television, along with print news media, from tabloid to serious journalism, provide a steady diet of apocalyptic imagery and belief, in catastrophic and utopian forms.

Rather than quelling the fear of endism and satisfying desire for electism, this consumption of the forms of expression seems to be generating insatiable craving for more. In light of that acceleration, I place this book in between the hope that millennial skepticism could curb apocalyptic appetites and the fear that it is too little, too late. To my mind, that in-between place is a kind of threshold, a place from which to peer, probe, and poke rather than prophesy. I often speak of the *turn* of the millennium because, as I see it from my constructed threshold, the date is arbitrary and apocalypticism dwells on either side. The "other side" of the third millennium is already inscribed in countless projects and plans on the side leading up to it. And vice versa—the apocalypticism that has found expression in the years leading up to the year 2000 is likely to continue in the years following. Given this cultural context, even a skeptic can reasonably surmise that for many these will be years of deep disappointment, for some a time of profound hope for a new era; for others, these will be years of renewed vigilance, and, for still others, years of ever-growing emptiness and apathy.

Apocalypse is a discourse that pronounces itself timeless. As a millennial skeptic, therefore, I am particularly concerned to acknowledge time and place. Apocalypse is a regime of truth that over many centuries has been especially oppressive toward women and racial and sexual minorities. In that light, each of these chapters is a concerted effort to demonstrate how this authoritarian regime continues through specific—that is, time-bound—issues of the day. Throughout, I strive to demythologize apocalypticism, putting the effects of millennialism on a concrete level. In seeking to understand certain current crises, ranging from debates on moral education to attacks on sexual freedom, my skeptical approach strives to expose the ways in which apocalypticism gallops over and buries complex history in the dust. Millennial skepticism is thus specifically geared to counter the momentum of an apocalyptic third millennium and its aftermath.

In the chapters that follow, I delineate what I mean by skeptical truth. While casting doubt on claims for absolute and universal Truth, I am simultaneously compelled to argue for skeptical activism. Chapter 1 is an effort to reappropriate the concept of revelation as a process of discovery based on personal experience, historical inquiry, and self-reflection. Skeptical revelation, in short, is a decidedly human process, not a transcendent illumination or vision from an all-knowing source. In that vein, I recount three visits to the island of Patmos and the process through which I determined to write this book.

Chapters 2 and 3 give pride of place to Tony Kushner's *Angels in America* as an illustration of what I mean by skeptical revelation. The phrase "threshold of revelation," found in both parts of *Angels*, resonated so profoundly for me that I have borrowed it for this Introduction and returned to it thematically in several chapters. Kushner's phrase became another way of articulating the perspective of skepticism that I regard as crucial for analyzing apocalyptic and millennialist belief. These two chapters are companion pieces, with the first endorsing skepticism as a valuable perspective in current debates about moral education and, indeed, for moral evaluation in general, and the second arguing for skepticism as a guide for theory. Issues of moral education and theory per se have come under a great deal of scrutiny over the last decade, which is welcome enough. Too often, however, the scrutinizers denounce certain moral stances and theoretical approaches from a position that assumes their exclusive hold on truth. These essays draw on *Angels* as a guide for skeptical thought about morality and theory at the turn of the millennium, a guide which dislodges dogmatic claims for absolute truth.

As I indicated before and as I hope these chapters make clear, my notion of skepticism is not an effort to duplicate the ancient Greek tradition. It strives instead to rearticulate skepticism for our own time. Chapter 3 therefore espouses Foucault's genealogical method as crucial to millennial skepticism but cautions against capitulating to apocalyptic categories. Apocalyptic motifs echo through Foucault's opposition between history and genealogy, with the forces of good—the genealogical gathering of multiple and contingent moments—promising to defeat those of evil—the monumental histories of linear cause and effect. Put simply, as a method, genealogy loses its effectiveness when it gets channeled into apocalyptic structures.

Chapter 4 explores how apocalyptic and millennialist truth gets incorporated, that is, literally embodied in various discourses, particularly from education and literature. Apocalyptic thought has always been intricately focused on sexuality, both through a sexualized rhetoric to express good and evil and through pronounced attention to sexual acts. Alarm over sexuality tends to intensify when cultural apocalypticism becomes more pervasive, as it does at the turn of a century and even more so at the turn of a millennium. The sound of this alarm has been amplified by the proliferation of sexually transmitted diseases and, most notably, the spread of AIDS worldwide. Within the United States, sexuality is playing a pivotal role as a site of struggle between theocratic and democratic forces. This chapter investigates efforts by the Religious Right to mandate abstinence-based sex education in public schools, efforts which were consolidated throughout the 1990s, gaining momentum from apocalyptic rhetoric and millennialist expectation. By considering Thoreau's espousal of chastity as an expression of skepticism about the naturalness of heterosexuality, I offer his way of thinking about chastity, which embraces rather than denounces sexuality, as an ethical challenge to the Right's dogmatism. In Thoreau's essays, as with Kushner's dramas, I highlight skeptical revelations that I hope might become meaningful within the politics of the body and the body politic.

Chapter 5 continues this examination of how millennialist concepts of chastity and purity become both embodied and politically charged. Here I focus on the Christian Right men's movement of the 1990s which emerged as an effort to reestablish biblically defined male authority in contemporary culture. My particular focus is on the Promise Keepers as the most effectively organized of these groups during the decade, until financial difficulties curtailed their momentum and forced them to rely more on volunteer efforts. The official status of the organization, notwithstanding, Promise Keepers beliefs have made an impact on a large number of American families. I show how their principal concept of purity depends on scapegoating feminists and homosexuals. I conclude by again pointing to *Angels in America* as a telling point of contrast, arguing that this two-part drama illuminates the ethical dilemmas and manifestations of violence that men in the United States face at the turn of the second millennium far more astutely than the writings and rallies of the Promise Keepers.

Chapter 6 is a response to political and cultural demands for sexual purity narrowly defined, one that "ups the ante" on resistance against apocalypticism and millennialism. From a perspective of millennial skepticism, apocalypse is a long-standing confidence game that breeds both gullibility and distrust. Building on the previous arguments about hatred of the Other inherent in apocalyptic thought, I underscore my view that such belief poses specific and often dire dangers to women. The current combination of apocalypticism and millennialism, I argue, is moving U.S. society toward crisis-oriented gender panic. To combat this, I wish to encourage affiliation with Jezebel, first by exposing the misogyny of portrayals of Jezebel in the Bible—portrayals that have considerable cultural resonance today in both religious and secular contexts—and then by joining her 2000 years later in her "blasphemy," for she dared to speak against the strictures of moral absolutism.

This chapter has an addendum that logs an experience located somewhere between vision and fantasy. It is a record of my embrace of Jezebelian skepticism as a fitting way to "carry on" as we begin the third millennium. The addendum is also a segue into the final chapter's focus on cybernetic technology. Although technology in and of itself is neither utopian nor dystopian, it is not neutral either. Its uses and consequences require careful consideration, particularly about the ways in which virtual technology as both a metaphor of the "New Era" and a socioeconomic practice is fraught with all too familiar real-world controversies regarding gender, sexuality, violence, and desire.

What happens when apocalyptic trepidation about destruction and millennialist desires for perfection join with forces of technology? My answer to that question is "technoppression." I have coined this term to describe how certain modes of technological power thrust toward domination. But, as with any power formation, the dominating elements of technoppression are concealed, most notably through millennialist rhetoric and techniques that promise perfection. Instead of the perfection promised through the coming of a messiah, this is a perfection programmed into bodies and promised as an outcome of cybernetic and virtual reality. We need to be as skeptical about programmed perfection as about millennialist perfection and, indeed, grasp the link between the two. To make this link more visible, I read the 1995 film *Strange Days* as an allegory of the postmodern era during which technoppression has taken hold.

Since ending is a slightly sticky problem for a book skeptical of stories about the End, I present an epilogue that is really another beginning, an opening to what I hope will be a lively cultural conversation in the third millennium. It is an effort to open up a sustained dialogue on skepticism as a way of life.

I, John . . . was in the isle that is
called Patmos.
—*The Book of Revelation (1:9)*

I SKEPTICAL
REVELATIONS
OF AN AMERICAN
FEMINIST ON
PATMOS

Plural, Partial, and Timely Revelations

The guide's hands directed my attention toward the crevices in
the stony wall as he intoned the words he had uttered countless times in
the Cave of the Apocalypse: "Here is where John rested his head. And
here the place he would put his hand to help hoist himself up from his
bed on the cave floor. The natural shelf against this wall, where the vest-
ment now hangs, served as a bookstand or table. These deep grooves in
the ceiling of the cave came from God's thundering voice when he spoke
to John. As you can see, it divided the top of the cave into three parts,
one for each of the divine trinity." Here I was, at last, in the place I had
thought about, often obsessed about, throughout my life, here where the
end of time itself was said to have been revealed in sound and image to
an elderly man named John, whose written record of the event has
shaped so much of human history.

My Catholic girlhood had given me vivid images of this place, a dark,
moist enclosure, suddenly and miraculously bursting with a radiant and
fiery light, followed by a series of Cecil B. de Mille sets: monstrous beasts

and dragon's breath, bodies in agony in a lake of fire, and then the city of jewels—gleaming like the Emerald City, as manicured as Tara before the war. Over the years, my indulgent Hollywood-bred imagination began to shift into another kind of grandeur in which martyred asceticism aligned me with John himself. Early adolescent fantasies mingled with Catholic shame and B-film depictions of wayward girls encouraged me to dissociate myself from that female path and instead to imagine myself as likely to be tapped for special honor as John himself.

By the time I got to college, there had been a supplanting of the metaphysics of much of this drama. Maybe I should say that the dramatic scripts of sexual tension remained recognizable but they were played out on a less metaphysical stage. My classes in religion were more devoted to the historical circumstances of John and Patmos and the first century of Christianity. The Jesuits at Loyola admitted discrepancies in texts while salvaging this odd biblical book as symbolically canonical. For me, the turn to history facilitated what would become several decades of rejection, not just of my religious upbringing but of all sorts of received ideas. Not that I moved all that far away from the dramatic rhythms of the Apocalypse and the egoistic grandeur of the Millennium. It is not difficult to see now that my involvements in the antiwar and civil rights movements and in feminism and Marxism had discarded the religious framework and yet retained its eschatological fervor. I believed we would overcome one day, to reign without discord.

Having become somewhat less convinced not only of this likelihood but also of the merit of its absolutism, I began writing *Anti-Apocalypse* during the first years of the 1990s. This process helped me grasp just how apocalyptic many social movements and theoretical perspectives are. My effort was to counter that tendency while still pursuing political and ethical alternatives.[1] What I was, and still am, most opposed to about apocalypticism is its insistence on absolute morality, theologically justified patriarchy, and preordained history with an (always imminent) End-time. Coupled with the electism of millennial belief, such conviction generates conspiracy thinking at its most reductive. Now, however, rather than stake out a primary stance in the oppositional "anti" camp, which tends to reenact a dollop and sometimes a heavy dose of the very apocalypticism it opposes, I am more inclined to pursue a stance that enables me to doubt apocalyptic and millennialist certainties and yet still make what I call "skeptical revelations." This does not mean that I am renouncing an antiapocalyptic perspective altogether. To the contrary, I remain convinced that a proliferation of oppositional perspectives is important for countering proponents of theocratic morality. Therefore I am still partial to what in *Anti-Apocalypse* I called "pissed criticism," which angrily targets the kind of righteousness that mandates its version of morality as the only acceptable one.

I mention these alterations and extensions of *Anti-Apocalypse* at this point to indicate that writing that book left me with too many questions about apocalypticism, what it has meant and continues to mean for the United States, and what it means for my own life. These considerations proved vexatious enough to spur this book as an attempt to understand how the present bears the hue of one millennium ending and another beginning. This book's efforts to assess the impact of the inception of a new millennium on deeply entrenched apocalyptic belief and actions needs further stipulation: In my focus on United States culture, I almost always deal with an apocalypticism that is either explicitly Christian or secular versions heavily informed by Christianity. As historians such as Ernest Tuveson and Sacvan Bercovitch have shown, belief in "America" and millennialism have long been intricately bound together.[2] Technically, the term *millennialism* refers to the belief that Christ will return, either before or after a thousand-year period, but millennialism as a cultural form is less focused on the precision of messianic return than it is on the messianic role of the nation itself. As Nathan Hatch has indicated, the conversion into "civil millennialism" helped galvanize forces on behalf of the American Revolution.[3] And as Paul Boyer and Stephen O'Leary have demonstrated, the appeal to apocalyptic and millennial righteousness is recurrent.[4]

What I want to stress is that millennialism, with its electism and expectation of perfected existence, is not only integral to contemporary U.S. life, it is dangerous to it. And, as a result of U.S. global relations, American millennialism endangers democratic practice around the world. This is not to gloss over the apocalyptic beliefs of other countries in which Catholic, Islamic, and Unification Church millennialism currently abound. There have been numerous instances of millenarianism (the belief in Christ's thousand-year return, regardless of the starting year) in Europe and elsewhere across the centuries. It is to stress that the use of "America" as an ideal, a colonizing goal, and a nationalist practice is uniquely and profoundly framed. In its current form, which is backed by digital technology and weaponry, U.S. techno-millennialism is an inordinately powerful force. Founded in the millennial spirit, motivated toward revolution through millennial drive, torn apart during the Civil War between forces equally convinced of their own millennialist rectitude, expanding as millennial empire over the twentieth century with an eye on the globe in the twenty-first century, America has apocalyptic gusto.

Attention to the year 2000, not just as the beginning of *a* new millennium but as the inception of *the* Millennium has readily fused with a nationalism built on millennial fervor. Indeed, the moniker "America 2000" became familiar, even routine, midway through the 1990s. That designation in turn heralds the bolder concept of "The American Millennium." Of course, this is the only millennium on the western calender for this and countless generations before and after to experience—and that is "a bit special," as the *Saturday Night Live* Church Lady says. But the exacerbation of millennial expectation around what many concede is an arbitrary date cannot simply be accounted for by the novelty of the three zeroes appearing only once every thousand years.[5]

Indeed, the idea of the third millennium as an American national product is a matter of consumption. By saying that U.S. society is consuming the millennium, I do not merely mean that it is relishing (in some cases binging on) the excitement of millennial belief, although certain segments seem to be doing so. Millennium T-shirts, watches, films, Television shows, cars, computers games, and plans for really big parties already abound.[6] But far more crucially, I mean that in the process of ingesting millennialism—by way of economic and cultural consumption—the United States is being consumed by it. One of the more literal versions of this process first appeared in *Christian Woman* magazine with two articles on the relationship between physical hunger and spiritual hunger. The "Weigh Down Workshop" weans overweight women from their overconsumption of fats and starches and replaces those inordinate desires for food (what author Gwendolyn K. Shamblin referred to as a "false god") with the reassurance that "He will fill you up." At a local church in my area, these articles were distributed to advertise a twelve-week seminar which, for the price of $103.00, promises to help women fight the "diet battle."[7] In this case, consuming the Bible is undertaken through a con- sumerized twelve-step program for weight reduction.

Even though most forms of consumption are not quite so faithful to the word, with this increasing commodification of American Christian- ity, especially through televangelism and huge entertainment-oriented churches, millennialist consumerism has grown exponentially. In many respects, the dividing line between religious and secular society is less visible than ever, with battles between separation of church and state ironically covering over the mutual transformation of each: the religios- ity of secular society and the secularization of religion. For this reason, I am arguing that in the United States, the upcoming millennium (a term which technically refers to any thousand-year designation, 1000, 2000, and so on) is inseparable from millennialism.

Apocalyptic intensification is endemic to this process of fusing the millennium with millennialism, which is being fed by three intertwined, ostensibly secular sources: transnational capitalist expansion of markets, technological acceleration of time, and postmodern heightening of feel- ings of being variously out of control, utterly controlled, or controlling. As a supersaturated idea with a commodity form naturalized by the cal- ender, *the* Millennium resonates with these intensities, directing them toward the promise of resolution even as its potent imagery exacerbates fear and apprehension. Furthermore, given the power of U.S. globaliza- tion, American millennialism is felt worldwide and shapes (sometimes reactively, at other times through missionary zeal) attitudes far beyond U.S. borders.[8] In this light, the debate about when the actual millennium is is a moot point. The contest between given dates—2000, 2001, two thousand years after Christ's birth, which probably means it has already happened, or as 2007, 2012, or 2033, according to various millenarian predictions for the End-time—not only extends the period of time for the production and consumption of millennium-inspired parapherna- lia, it also enlarges the arena of apocalyptic furor.

What, then, does reaching the beginning of the third millennium mean to U.S. citizens here and now? That depends in part on where one already stands. Part of the power of millennialism is precisely that it is capable of meaning different things to different groups, all the while extending its ideological hold by espousing America as *the* millennialist nation. For corporations, it opens new markets. For premillennialists, or Christian fundamentalists, it is the beginning of the end, when the forces of darkness are gathering their fury in war and plague and natural disasters; these believers find hope amidst this catastrophe in their personal salvation and some expect to be "raptured" at the onset of "tribulation." For many secular-minded apocalypticists, it marks everything from a rise in UFO sightings and abductions to doomsday scenarios like asteroid bombardment to growth in intergalactic cosmic harmony.[9] For politicians, it provides rhetorical trumpets for the American way. For me as a cultural critic skeptical about any inherent significance in either the year 2000 or spans of 1000 years in general, it means studying, with fascination and some apprehension, the *effects* of millennialism on a society mired in its structures of fear, hatred, hope, and zealotry.

That is largely why, a year after the publication of *Anti-Apocalypse*, I made my way to Patmos, or, to borrow John's phraseology, why I, Lee, "was in the isle that is called Patmos," exactly 1900 years after his startling encounter with sounds and images of timeless space. Separated by so many centuries and a multitude of life differences, our reasons for being on Patmos were decidedly dissimilar—though, as the account above indicates, clearly not unrelated. John's stay, while probably not outright exile, was the result of bearing witness to Jesus Christ under the duress of Roman rule. My travel had been aided by the auspices of both the U.S. Fulbright agency and funding from my home institution. But I was there because of John and my abiding fascination with his Book of Revelation and the repercussions of apocalyptic thought on U.S. society as we venture toward a third millennium.

Although I did not witness anything comparable to John's fabulous figures of chaos and triumph, I did have some revelations, then and subsequently. Some I have written down to make this book. Unlike John's Revelation, which ends with an admonishment that "if any man shall add unto these things, God shall add unto him the plagues that are written in this book" (22:18), I hope my revelations will prompt others to make additions to and alterations in my thought—to place it under doubt, to ascertain its merits or mistakes, and to determine when its time is up. In contrast to John's singular and divine Revelation, skeptical revelations are plural, lower-case, and meant to be timely. They are partial in both senses of the word—invariably incomplete and boldly committed to the merits of skepticism. Rather than announcing the end of time, they point toward the importance of timeliness, of being time-bound, grounded in time, and most of all, of enacting timely analysis and timely activism. As a mode of investigation, skeptical revelation defies endeavors to discredit quotidian existence and replace it with eternal bliss, whether from the Religious Right, the New Age Left, or commodity Capitalism. As a political stance, it aims to diffuse end-of-the-millennium fears and expectations that can easily trip into panic and violence.

Who Tells the Truth of the Millennium?

Patmos these days is as much a tourist spot as a place of holy pilgrimage, or as Batman's friend Robin might put it: "Holy Tourism!" I invoke Robin here for a particular reason: What I discovered on Patmos was that John had a "Robin" too. His name was Prochorus. Before saying more about Prochorus, let me back up a bit to return to the cave and narrate the circumstances of the first revelation I had there. My initial visit to Patmos lasted only a few hours. I arrived at the tag end of the unique kind of spectacle that has emerged within religious arenas in our own time as we sally into the third millennium. This was in April of 1995, just after the Greek Orthodox Easter celebrations. Like other postmodern religious festivities, especially in high aesthetic Christian circles, the Orthodox Easter services are a remarkable blend of pastoral nostalgia, magnificent pageantry, and media savvy. Adding to the usual heightening of excitement of the religious holiday was Patmos's unique celebration of the 1900th anniversary of John's vision.

With my older sister Miriam Simpson as my companion, I hopped aboard the tour bus at 7:30 on a misty morning and listened to the friendly, albeit stilted, bus guide relate the key dates and architectural highlights of the island. My sister's presence was especially important in regard to my visit to Patmos. Six years younger, I have always felt like a Robin to her Batman maturity and intelligence. Over the years we had grown apart. For knowledge of each other's lives, we relied on communication from our mother. As a result, although I knew when important events occurred in my sister's life, I was unaware of how she felt and what she thought about them. As for myself, I had always assumed that she would have little interest in my life. This trip allowed that to change, in part because I had written about apocalypticism and so felt, for the first time in my life, more her partner in conversation. But it was not the content or informational element that really had significance. Rather, it was the emotional connection. From that developing bond, I have come to realize just how crucial emotion is to knowledge. In saying this, I am not taking up the banner of confessional discourse. Instead, I am saying that skeptical revelation entails seeing both emotion and cognition as not only time and culture bound, but also bound together. This feminist insight offers an important corrective to the otherwise overly abstract concept of power/knowledge, which though vital to cultural analysis, tends to ignore the psychological and emotional links that foster and constrain us as knowing subjects.

A twenty-minute bus ride up a winding road from the port city Skala brought us to the entrance of the starkly white-washed Monastery of the Revelation. After descending several sets of stairs, I paused for a moment to read the epigram posted in Greek and English above the entrance door: "How fearful this place is!" One by one, the group I was with entered the darkened grotto, now divided between the cave on one side and the chapel of Saint Anne on the other. It takes a moment for the eyes to adapt from the dazzling sun-drenched walls to this shadowy interior, lit only by candles and the shimmer of gold on the altar and the wall paintings and icons that adorn the site of John's vision. I was surprised that, rather than feeling fearful as prompted, I felt pleasurably serene in this setting and so opted to sit awhile on the bench that is set up parallel to the wall against which John is said to have slept, letting my eyes wander over the various images as the guide's voice drifted through my mind.

As I took in the details of what happened that fateful day when John had his vision, suddenly my attention became riveted on one of the paintings. There, near where John's feet would have been, is an icon by Thomas Vathas, circa 1596. In the lower right-hand portion is a figure I had never seen in any Protestant or Catholic depiction of the Apocalypse. John is there, of course, haloed and framed by an arched cave entrance. He sits on a rocky chair, his body inclined toward the right as his head cranes away from the cave. One hand rests on his knee, the other helps hold his head as he stares off into space. But John is not alone. Across from him, perched on an L-shaped bench, is a haloed young man fast at work writing on a scroll. The writing stops halfway down, with white space filling the remaining part of the scroll.

When I first caught sight of this painting, my mind swirled with confusion. John had a scribe? I asked my sister if she had ever seen a painting of John with a scribe; her answer was no. My Catholic-school theology classes whizzed through my memory but I could not come up with a single mention of anyone but John himself recording his vision. I had read a great number of studies of the Apocalypse while writing *Anti-Apocalypse*, and no one ever said anything about another person either being present at the time of the vision or afterward to write it down for John. And I had pored over the Book of Revelation—John certainly never mentions anyone else. Indeed, the text gives quite the opposite impression with the warning: "For I testify unto everyman that heareth the words of the prophecy of this book, if any man shall add unto these things, God shall add unto him the plagues that are written in this book: And if any man shall take away from the words of the book of this prophecy, God shall take away his part out of the book of life, and out of the holy city, and from the things which are written in this book" (Revelation 22: 18–19). Of course that does not preclude a scribe, just warn him that he better get it exactly right. When I asked my guide, she seemed disgruntled to have to linger at the site, but when pressed she agreed to ask the more official cave guide. He responded with a matter-of-factness borne of absolute faith: "This is Prochorus, John's disciple, to whom John dictated his vision." More questions elicited no more information, only reiteration.

Slightly agitated from the disruption over what I had thought I had known, I looked around the cave and discovered yet another depiction of the two men, this one actually painted on the wall of the cave toward the end of the twelfth century. Again, there was Prochorus, writing intently, and John, this time standing above him, eyes cast toward heaven, hands without scroll or writing implement. Racing back up the monastery staircases to the tables of booklets and souvenirs, I purchased all of the English visitors' guides and monastery histories I could find. Much to my delight (my own apocalyptic gusto clearly on display here), a whole handful of kitsch items were also available—miniatures of John and Prochorus on icons and painted rocks for paperweights. And then my tour bus whisked me, my sister, and the other pilgrim-tourists away to the Monastery of St. John, a medieval fortress that towers over the island. And here, too, in the monastery's museum and treasury room, amidst any number of exquisite paintings of John, either in the form of iconic portrait or a more elaborately filled canvas with the heavens opening up to reveal to him their glory, was another painting featuring my "mystery man." This one was an illuminated manuscript miniature from 1334–35, bearing the museum designation, "St. John the Divine dictates to Prochorus."

My first skeptical revelation, then, is that sometimes truth has to be undone and that that process is as much emotional as it is mental. By no means had I gone to Patmos as a believer. Not of divine Truth anyway. But I began to see that, despite thinking I had rejected the mythology of the Apocalypse, I remained immersed in certain beliefs that I had received from an education almost exclusively geared to Western Christianity. I had never even heard of this young man whom Greek Orthodox Christians celebrated. Of course I knew well enough from my own espousal of multicultural education that U.S. schooling is inadequate when it comes to teaching about other cultures. But too often the solution amounts to overlaying one's own assumption on those of other cultures, as indeed I had. What became clear in a more concrete way was that unlearning is requisite to new learning. For me, this revelation was enabled by the relationship my sister and I were forging. It was induced by our growing emotional ties which paralleled and depended on our own process of unlearning and learning family knowledge. Whether it involves family or cultural history, unlearning memory can be emotionally wrenching. So too, emotional receptivity seems to me to be intimately linked to gaining new knowledge.

Dropping my exclusive focus on John in order to discover more about Prochorus, I eagerly turned to the visitor's guidebooks. This was frustrating at best. All I could cull from these sources were bits and pieces of information which completely fuse the historical and the theological—a distinction that I acknowledge does not make any sense from the standpoint of one who believes history to be a divine unfolding. Nevertheless, what I was able to garner clearly from this cross-cultural encounter is the extent of conflict among the historical records. Both Greek Orthodox and Western Christian fundamentalist sources claim the John of the Revelation to be the same John as the disciple, whereas Western secular sources argue that John was not the same as the disciple, but, rather, a charismatic preacher of the Jesus sect.[10] Neither the religious nor the secular western sources mention Prochorus anywhere. The Western Christian fundamentalist tradition sticks to the text of Revelation, pretty much ignoring John's life on Patmos prior to the Revelation and afterward, except to say that he returned to Ephesus to die. The Greek Orthodox booklets not only emphasize John's performance of miracles but also Prochorus's record-keeping of them. They cite John's miraculous premonition of his own death and the manna that exuded from his tomb and cured the afflicted. According to one of the Greek Orthodox pamphlets, Prochorus was with John during the time of John's fasting and prayer that led up to the Revelation and when, more crucially, "The Great Visionary of Patmos, obedient to the divine command, began to dictate to his disciple Prochorus his account of the appearance of the Lord in majesty."[11]

When I returned to Patmos about six weeks later, I was able to stay for several days and explore the terrain a little. Patmos is a starkly barren island, with masses of stone jutting abruptly out of the sea, which shimmers deep-blue against the rock, occasionally turning turquoise in the inlets that punctuate the irregular coastline. The summer heat and glare is merciless. One early afternoon, I retraced the mountainous path that John himself had probably walked from his cave down to the sea. As heat exhaustion overtook me, my head throbbed so violently that I expected—half hoped for, half feared—some kind of vision, at least a hallucination if not a visitation from a divine intermediary. In keeping with my ambivalence, I was sorely disappointed and just as keenly relieved. No images filled the sky, uncanny or supernatural, and no voices surrounded me except for that of my friend, Kate Mehuron, whose greater athleticism was clearly paying off.

Upon my return to the hotel, my exhaustion was rewarded with a kind of inspiration, the little revelations that writers are grateful for, because they provide bursts of energy and direction: "Truth is *Prochorean!*" My second revelation on Patmos, then, is that skepticism promotes an understanding of how truth is established, or to put it more aptly in this context, inscribed. A good deal of this revelation has to be credited to the conversations that Kate and I had just had as we trudged along in the sweltering heat. The dialogical nature of revelatory thought is customarily played down, however. John does not give it (or himself) its due in the Book of Revelation. Instead, he credits Jesus' word as total, entirely distinct from anything he himself might have contributed. And this, of course, is the paradigm of so much aesthetic theory that privileges monological originality over dialogical richness.

Saying that truth is Prochorean stands as a stark contrast. It means that truth itself is dialogical. Not that I think that any of the island legends about Prochorus or the medieval paintings depicting him with scroll in hand had such a notion in mind. But their portrayals do complicate the status of truth. Who, after all, is telling the truth of the Apocalypse if it is mediated not just once but twice? Prochorean truth highlights what John conceals, namely, his own role in recording what he sees and hears from his source. And with one glimpse of Prochorus as scribe, this complication is doubled with the dictation extending from one human source to another. In making dialogics a foundation of truth, Prochorean style, skepticism stands as a reminder that truth is attained and revealed through communication with the thoughts of others. And, although there is no reason to think that the name *Prochorus* has allegorical significance for Greek Orthodoxy, I am enchanted by the etymological link that *pro* and *chorus* has for English speakers, as if affirming dialogics by putting forward a chorus of voices.

When I returned to the United States and was taken up by teaching and writing more of this book, the concept of truth as Prochorean continued to intrigue me. But various complications came to mind about how I might approach it and with them, ironically, came a form of self-intimidation that seems to plague academic inquiry. The antithesis of Prochorean truth appears in that self-doubting internal voice that persecutes thought, haughtily asking, "Hasn't all this already been said, indeed been said more profoundly and cleverly by Derrida and Foucault, not to mention the scads of academics who have rearticulated their insights?" And so I put off writing about truth as Prochorean for the time being even though the idea continued to play around in my head. This is the other side of dialogics, a reminder of why we should not romanticize it: negatively disposed internalized voices can enter the dialogical dynamic too.

In July 1996, I returned for a two-week stay, still determined to unearth more of the mystery of Prochorus and to learn more about the island where he had lived, for in the course of the year I had begun to think of Patmos less as John's island and more as the place where Prochorus lived and wrote. My friend Bessie Dendrinos accompanied me to the cave and the monastery this time, listening attentively to the intricacies of this inquiry. She then interviewed the Director of the Ecclesiastical School about Prochorus, translating back and forth for both of us between English and Greek. Through that interview I have made some headway in figuring out what is known about Prochorus. With Bessie's help, I was able to learn about his status as a saint in the Greek Orthodox Church and the manuscript that is pseudonymously attributed to him. I also knew by then that there was one reference to a Prochorus in the New Testament, in the Acts of the Apostles, when the apostles choose seven disciples, among them one named Prochorus, to help them in their ministry. It made sense, then, that the late-dated text be designated under the name of one of these men. Probably written in the fifth century, *Journeys of St. John the Divine* is not only an apocryphal text but also the source of much of the legend around both men. It tells, for example, about John's defeat of Cynops, a pagan sorcerer or magician on Patmos. In one such contest, Cynops leapt into the water to bring a drowned man back to life, but John made the sign of the cross over him and Cynops himself drowned. What I ultimately gathered from these translation sessions is that the records of official history are in such conflict about Prochorus's existence that the only sure conclusion to draw is that his history is and probably always will be an incomplete record, complicated by insufficient record keeping, religious conviction, and the power/knowledge relations that perpetuate legend.

Disappointing though that might sound, it is really the basis of yet another revelation that came my way during my most recent stay on

Patmos: the pursuit of truth is an activity of transcribing inevitably incomplete information. The emphasis on process here is part of the first revelation which upholds the relationship between unlearning and learning, for what I now call revelations are the realizations I gain along the way when I have committed myself to figuring something out—whether I solve the problem or not. Of course, that idea has been around for a long time too and articulated more brilliantly by others. Acknowledging that is part of the second revelation having to do with Prochorean truth and its dialogical nature. Prochorean truth gives pride of place to the dialogical dynamic which refuses to foreclose on the "already said." The truth that is being told may have been inscribed elsewhere by other thinkers, but value resides in its reinscription, which makes it subject to change as it is presented, really re-presented, to someone else in another time and a different place, with its own effects.

From this perspective, even though he is "just a scribe," Prochorus is less circumscribed by his master than his master is in insisting that he has received and passed on the Truth as total, complete, and forever the same. These insights led to my third revelation: skepticism insists that the recording of truth is always an act of *tran*scription, or translation. A skeptical revelation of truth, in other words, acknowledges itself as an act of interpretation for a new context. In my mind's eye, Prochorus, the lovely young man bent over his unfinished scroll, is writing, as best he can, what he understands as truth, translating God's word to John and John's word to him so that it might be read by others. This last revelation is what encouraged me to take up Prochorus's position, with my computer screen as an always unfinished scroll, and to present this book as skeptical truth, a web of dialogical and dynamic knowledge that seeks to confront and challenge claims to dictated and timeless Truth.

The categories of good and evil are no longer
viable objects of thought. What would it be like
to live a life without—not in defiance of—these
categories?
—Adam Phillips, "Besides Good and Evil"

2 TEACHING ON THE THRESHOLD: *ANGELS* AND SKEPTICS

Part of the deepening crisis in education today centers on a debate over what is often called moral education. Lots of folks across the political spectrum, it seems, are for it, but what they mean by moral education varies widely. For some, it means that creationism should be taught instead of evolution. For others, it means marshalling campaigns against alcohol and drug abuse. My own view as an educator is that working against threats to democratic freedom—such as sexism, racism, and homophobia—should be a crucial component of education. Rather than regarding such conflicting views as a crisis, however, I see this debate as one that can potentially strengthen education precisely because it forces a reconsideration of the category of the moral. To fortify that reconsideration, we would do well to ask the question that Adam Phillips has posed about both the traditional and the Nietzschean antithesis of good versus evil: "What have we used the conflict between good and evil to stop ourselves thinking?"[1]

Perhaps more than any other topic, apocalypse, especially at the beginning of a new millennium, highlights some of the problems inherent to the issue of moral education. The formulation of the end of the world dramatizes two of the key—but not always directly addressed—questions of moral education: Why be moral—and how? The Book of Revelation justifies strict moral compliance through threats of destruction incomparable in its merciless vengeance and glorious promise of divine reward. Although this apocalyptic-minded morality is justifiably part of the debate, it is also part of the problem for a pluralistic society in which separation of church and state is constitutionally mandated. In the context of public education, what becomes clear is that a monolithically prescriptive moral code which depends on a metaphysical rationale for conduct, truth, or judgment is inimical to the needs of a multicultural democratic society. Any form of pedagogical electism, regardless of its political affiliation, endangers democratic process. And yet, the question returns: Isn't the exploration of morality crucial to democratic education?

From my pedagogical perspective, the problemization of the moral and a fostering of social criticism are the principal components of democratic education. This is best understood as a stance of skepticism, since it seeks to cast doubt on certainty itself, most crucially certainty about absolute morality and universal truth which function through the categories of good versus evil. Skepticism also places the many possible responses to both the why and the how of morality under scrutiny. My focus is on teaching apocalypse, but the stance I am proposing applies to other fields of knowledge as well and extends beyond the classroom. Of course espousing skepticism in debates on moral education is simpler said than done, especially given current polarizations of academic life. It would be naive not to acknowledge some of the liabilities entailed in such an effort. The theocratic momentum in the United States at the turn of the millennium is fraught with threats to freedom of thought, speech, and action in the name of "higher" morality. In certain academic settings, teaching from a perspective of millennial skepticism could mean getting fired or endlessly entangled in legal hassles. The danger of orthodoxy is precisely the best defense of skepticism as a means of supporting academic freedom. It is also the case that secular moralists who insist on absolute truth and reductive politics view skepticism as a "cop out." Part of its value is to steer away from that position, which also thwarts freedom of thought and practice and has been exacerbated by the millennialism of our culture. And finally, skepticism is sometimes misunderstood as a form of relativism which aggravates an already alarming slide into moral apathy and cynicism. But one of skepticism's values is the way it questions that stance too.

Positioning oneself pedagogically as a skeptical moral agent and knower is akin to being precariously perched on what Tony Kushner has called the "threshold of revelation."[2] The key word in Kushner's felicitous phrase is *threshold*, because to step over the threshold—to teach from "on high," from a place of presumed revelation of absolute truth (whether metaphysical or empirical, politically right, center, or left)—curbs the freedom of thought and speech foundational to democratic education. Teaching apocalypse from a skeptical perspective makes the classroom a site of inquiry about truth, power relations, and freedom rather than one of moral and epistemological rectitude. On either side of the threshold is the seduction of certainty; on one side lurks the revelation of scientism and on the other that of metaphysics. The skepticism of the threshold probes both of these forms of revelation, examining their assumptions and conclusions and analyzing their dogmatic insistences.

I invoke Kushner in particular because I began to think of teaching as a threshold place when I used both parts of his play *Angels in America* as the final texts in a first-year seminar called "Apocalypse."[3] I teach at Hobart and William Smith Colleges, a small liberal arts institution in upstate New York that, I am happy to say, has made gender awareness, cultural difference, and ethical thinking explicit goals of its curriculum. My course was one section of a General Education requirement for fifteen entering students. Students had chosen it from thirty such sections, each reflecting the instructor's own particular scholarly and pedagogical interests. As I write this essay, I have taught the Apocalypse seminar three times, most recently for members of the class of 2001.

When Kushner's *Angels* entered my classroom, teaching on the threshold of revelation became paramount. Kushner introduces the phrase "threshold of revelation" in Act I of *Part One: Millennium Approaches* when two of the main characters, Prior Walter, a man with AIDS whose lover is about to leave him, and Harper Pitt, a woman who has become addicted to valium as a response to her husband's rejection of her, suddenly find themselves together in a "mutual dream scene." Kushner stages the scene as a kind of magical realism in which the two characters interact in proximity with one another despite the fact that, at that very moment, they are living quite separate lives in different locales.

The scene is a little bit like a classroom. As teachers, we meet our students—and they us and each other—as strangers. Having lived vastly disparate lives, there we are, suddenly together discussing issues of life-and-death importance. What Harper says about her drug-induced hallucinations applies equally to this gathering of intimate strangers: "This is the very threshold of revelation sometimes. You can see things." *Angels* reminds us that we can see *some* things, often heretofore covered-up things, but not *every* thing. Teaching on the threshold encourages revelations of all sorts of knowledge but discourages the belief that teachers dispense *the* Revelation. Just as standing sideways on a threshold affords a view of where we came from and where we might be headed, teaching skeptically can make visible the ending of one way of thinking and the beginning of another. Thresholders can see both ways, but the view is nonetheless limited in range. Skepticism thus makes the classroom a kind of limit place—a threshold or boundary—of knowledge, demarcating the physical and metaphysical.

This is particularly acute when the topic of teaching is apocalypse, where endings and beginnings are foregrounded in unique ways. The vagaries of history usually help maintain a skeptical perspective by showing how beliefs travel and change through commerce and/or exile. Thus also teaching can become a threshold of revelation by fostering a stance of skepticism in regard to biblical apocalypse as a practical and ethical matter, because insisting on any one truth would necessarily crush someone else's belief. Needless to say, this is a complex negotiation; students in a given class may well include, as mine did, Christian next to Islamic fundamentalists, Jews, Catholics, religious atheists and ufologists, to name only a few of the possible communities of belief.

The (admittedly difficult to maintain) position of skepticism that I am advocating is committed to tracing the contours of apocalyptic thought, its historical emergence in ancient cultures and manifestations in contemporary culture, and its effects on individuals and societies. On this view, teaching about apocalypse extends to the ways in which beliefs about the origin and end of time inform literature, law, science, philosophy, feminism, history, and popular culture. Each of these fields of knowledge benefits from the threshold stance as well. As a place neither inside revelation nor oblivious to it, the threshold is a position from which one can analyze the historical events and social forces that have given shape and substance not just to these fields of knowledge but to the very objects they study, often otherwise seen as the natural givens or universals of experience. In this regard, a threshold is a place cognizant of the workings of power, through which physiological and psychological effect occurs on both the individual and societal level. This is, again, a skeptical position, since apocalyptic belief assumes and proclaims tenets of universal human nature and absolute truth. Teaching on the threshold thus requires a willing acceptance of uncertainty, hardly an easy task, but one, I think, salutary as a pedagogical principle.

Indeed, even to choose *Angels in America* for a course on apocalypse makes manifest the ways in which relations of power and knowledge intersect. Controversy surrounds the play because of its focus on homosexuality and its nudity. When I introduced it to my students, I xeroxed two newspaper clippings that exemplified this point, one on the decision at Catholic University in Washington, D.C., to ban advertisement of a student production of the play and not to allow the performance to take place in the university's campus theater, and another on the unsuccessful effort by the Christian Right to prohibit its performance in Charlotte, North Carolina. I also pointed out that academic critical controversy, by contrast, has centered more on the question of whether the play, especially Part II, ultimately betrays its radical vision, or as David Savran put it, has "accommodated with stunning ease to the hegemonic ideology not just of the theater-going public, but of the democratic majority—an ideology that has become the *new* American religion—liberal pluralism."[4]

Although individual students, and I as the teacher, might agree with either of these positions or hold that Kushner fosters something else altogether, resolution was not the goal. All of these positions deserve discussion within the classroom and analysis of their implications. The threshold perspective endorses debate, which can get pretty heated under certain circumstances, in place of consensus. Rather than trying to resolve the conflict, therefore, after airing as many differing positions as possible, we discussed how this cultural debate highlights an ongoing one in the United States between theocratic and democratic decision making. The main role I undertook in this discussion was to ascertain the implications of each position and to stress that a skeptical stance in regard to truth and morality need not lead to a do-nothing position as citizens, pointing out that this is one of the themes of the play itself.

Because of its advocacy of a skepticism that includes social criticism as essential to moral citizenry, *Angels in America* provides a remarkable guide for how to think about apocalypticism from this venturesome threshold place. Kushner turns the elements of apocalyptic belief around and over to disclose surprising edges of humor and poignant implications. He also exposes complicity in brutality in apocalyptic belief, indicating how its images of divine devastation have been used to justify human destruction. Ultimately, *Angels* fosters a vision of America and self that partakes of the urgency of an apocalyptic sense of loss and hope without augmenting moral absolutism or exacting violence against others. The final lines of *Part Two: Perestroika*, spoken by Prior Walter in his fifth year of living with AIDS, encapsulate this threshold vision:

> This disease will be the end of many of us, but not nearly all, and the dead will be commemorated and will struggle on with the living, and we are not going away. We won't die secret deaths anymore. The world only spins forward. We will be citizens. The time has come. Bye now.
> You are fabulous creatures, each and every one.
> And I bless you: *More life.*
> The Great Work Begins.[5]

These words are spoken to the audience in a tone prophetically reminiscent of the Book of Revelation, but unlike John's characterization of his own response when confronted by angels, Prior has not fallen, as if struck dead or to worship, at the feet of the angel (Revelation 1:17). Nor does he claim to be a solitary seer, as John does. Instead, along with his friends Louis, Hannah, and Belize, all sitting together on the rim of the Bethesda Fountain in Central Park, they have just collectively—I would call it Prochorean style—told the story of the angel Bethesda who descended to the Temple Square in Jerusalem where a fountain "shot up from the ground" when her "foot touched earth." Having run dry when the Romans destroyed the temple, the fountain is to flow again "When the Millennium comes."[6]

Woven around the telling of this belief is a conversation comprised of diverse and even conflicting points of view about the place of theory as explanation and prescription. There is no effort to diminish or subsume the dissenting claims in the name of consensus. The play's closing words thus proffer a way of viewing existence that is neither totalistic nor nihilistic: "*More Life.*" This Hebrew word for blessing is uttered on the threshold between promises of peace and portents of appalling suffering, given the momentous and calamitous world events of 1990, the year this scene takes place: the fall of the Berlin Wall, Perestroika, the breakup of Yugoslavia, and ongoing battles between Palestine and Israel. It is precisely within this incessant whirl of hope and despair that the admonition for "more life" can serve as a model for skeptical moral education.

Since bringing *Angels in America* into the classroom means focusing intensely on issues of gender, race, and sexuality—all recurrent elements of apocalypticism—it is important to create a foundation of thought that is both historically and culturally astute. In my first-year seminar on "Apocalypse," these issues are grounded by using the Book of Revelation as the first text followed by Norman Cohn's genealogy of apocalyptic belief in the ancient world, Paul Boyer's historical and sociological treatment of prophecy belief, Tina Pippin's feminist analysis of Revelation, Hal Lindsey's *The Late Great Planet Earth* as indicative of fear of the Other (including orientalism, racism, and anti-semitism), and Charles Strozier's study of the psychology of Christian fundamentalism.[7]

Starting with the Book of Revelation is a way of indicating that—even though many people in the United States haven't read it (most of my students have not, though the few who have know it extremely well)—it has nonetheless permeated U.S. culture. In preparation for discussion, I ask students to bring in both a performative and written (explanatory) response to their reading. In my three years of teaching this course, I have been introduced to any number of rock songs, comic books, literary works, and films in which they have detected, many for the first time, key images and themes of Revelation. Some choose to paint an image themselves. On one occasion, a small group prepared a dance routine that expressed the drama of impossible escape from divine wrath. As a first assignment, this functions as an ice-breaking exercise, but more importantly, it clarifies for the group that, at least in regard to individual and popular interpretations, there is no single meaning to the text.

From there, the emphasis shifts to Norman Cohn's historical treatment of ancient belief systems in which he points out certain links between divine warriors in various ancient combat myths and the Messiah of Revelation. Although Cohn's work is difficult for first-year students (so are the other books), it is invaluable for several reasons. For one thing, it provides knowledge of distinctive, internally logical systems of moral belief that lasted for thousands of years. For another, his argument about the contingent effects of Zoroastrianism on Judaism and early Christianity dispels the notion of cultural unity by showing how cultural migrations alter both colonizers and colonized. The writing assignment is geared toward elucidating his argument rather than evaluating it, in part because students don't yet have sufficient scholarly information to either refute or agree with him, and in large part because I want them to learn how to articulate someone else's ideas accurately and succinctly—a crucial skill for moral problemization.

The next readings combine historical with rhetorical analysis. Paul Boyer's book surveys prophecy belief from its earliest enactments up through current expression in the United States, with some focus on the tension in premillennialism regarding the representation of Jews. We also read Hal Lindsey's famous fundamentalist text in concert with Boyer's analysis of it and Tina Pippin's feminist analysis of the complex ways in which Revelation depicts feminine figures as either idealized or demonized. Two films help make these discussions more concrete. *The Atomic Cafe* provides ample evidence of apocalyptic rhetoric and accusation at a host of "others." And *The Seventh Sign* illustrates Pippin's general contention about idealization, with Demi Moore's character, Abby Quinn, as a messianic mother figure who must sacrifice herself to save the world from apocalyptic destruction. My experience has been that discussion becomes more intense at this point, with students becoming somewhat polarized and defensive, especially around gender issues. The writing assignment asks them to explore Boyer's and Pippin's positions more thoroughly by examining the tension in the representation of women and Jews in premillennialist thought. Here I make it very clear that they don't have to agree with the argument they will be making about this tension. The point is to write a coherent account that criticizes depictions of alterity, or otherness. Part of class discussion centers on learning the skill of constructing a coherent argument from a perspective one might disagree with. The merit of this exercise is borne out because the students who characterize themselves as nonfeminist tend to write the most logical, coherent essays in response to this feminist assignment.

The class then turns to the emotional effects of belief in an imminent End. I have found Charles Strozier's treatment particularly helpful in guiding me and my students through what he calls the "mindset of endism." Students report in their evaluations that this is a course favorite, seeing it as both accessible and fairminded; Strozier's unusual blend of dramatic "case study" narratives and cultural analysis makes this work less dry in their view. Its value for skeptical moral education derives largely from the way he accords respect to the various Christian funda-mentalists he has interviewed while also illuminating the totalistic fea-tures of Christian fundamentalist belief. The book's cross-cultural focus, which has chapters on Hopi and New Age apocalypticism, provides evi-dence that apocalyptic belief can be far less totalistic than it tends to be in Christian fundamentalist form. The writing assignment asks for a com-parison/contrast discussion of these forms of endist belief.

By the time we get to Kushner's work, students have become mindful not only of the normative beliefs structural to apocalypticism but also to the dramatically divergent personal and societal effects of various apoc-alyptic belief systems over time. From each of these scholarly studies, they have learned to discern the function of binary thought within apocalyptic discourse, in particular the pitting of good against evil. The binary structure of apocalypse is the most fixed element of its normative morality. Cohn importantly allows them to see the particular way that this binary concept came to be linked with monotheism and a belief in a deferred afterlife. Pippin shows the ways in which this opposition gets expressed in terms of gender, with values associated with masculinity being privileged over those of femininity. Boyer demonstrates the ways in which Christian fundamentalism divides the redeemed from the unredeemed along religious, sexual, and ethnic lines; his chapter on

Lindsey's book becomes more concrete when they read about such things as "the yellow peril" first hand. Strozier, finally, shows how strict adherence to apocalyptic binaries of good versus evil, burdened as they are with justifications of destruction, can result in psychic breaks like dissociation and doubled narratives of selfhood.

These authors also stress, however, that apocalyptic belief has at times also seriously challenged oppressive regimes of morality, ranging from the Jewish and Christian struggles against persecution in the ancient world to liberation theology in our own time. A belief in the end of the world as we know it has sustained myriad battles for freedom over the centuries. *Angels* incorporates both this critique and advocacy of apocalypticism. My students tell me that Kushner's work both unsettles and puts in place what they have learned up to that point. This is not surprising because most of them are generally unfamiliar with what Kushner calls a "gay fantasia." More crucially, however, I think it is because they are unaccustomed to examining the meaning of morality. *Angels* helps us to see that, at its best, moral education undertakes to do just that. Questioning the value of obedience to rigid moral tenets, Kushner shifts emphasis to the moral relationships a person can develop—with him- or herself, with friends and lovers, and with one's nation. With those issues in mind, I ask students to write their final essay on the ethical development of one of the characters from the play.

Among the play's many challenges to dogmatic morality, one of the most spirited (forgive the pun) is its examination of patriarchal masculinity. This is probably why so many of my students, male and female, choose one of the male characters for their focus. Although the play extends to any number of such complex reevaluations, I want to delineate that theme here in particular not only because it highlights the harm associated with certain apocalyptic beliefs being promoted in the United States today but also because it prompts consideration of a countermorality. (In Chapter 5, I more fully discuss the danger of apocalyptic masculinity). Through the characters of Prior Walter, Louis Ironson, and Belize, Kushner makes concrete what it means for men to live within a society that makes them feel like God has abandoned them, a society in which one's sexuality is said to justify condemnation and punishment. When Prior discovers that he has AIDS, he is forced to confront crucial questions involving personal and societal morality. What makes life worth living? How is he to go on when his body is wracked with the pain of disease? When his lover turns away in disgust and deserts him because he cannot cope with the suffering before him? Through Louis Ironson and Joe Pitt, *Angels* explores the emotional costs of abandonment on the one who has abandoned a lover or spouse. Roy Cohn's character, in return, demonstrates how social ostracism can turn inward to create self-hatred so strong that it retaliates with shocking cruelty. By portraying Joe Pitt's compliance with Cohn's crimes, Kushner raises questions about what ordinary men should do when powerful men such as Cohn are stridently self-serving, willing to inflict unsparing harm on others.

The self-hatred and denials of emotion that ensue from forging a masculinity that equates manhood with heterosexuality, condemnation of homosexuality, and Christian nationalism are represented in the character of Joe Pitt. Joe personifies the form of apocalyptic belief that has come to unite America and traditional family values. As a Mormon, he has inculcated an absolutistic morality that threatens everlasting punishment for homosexuals. As a young Republican lawyer, he has learned blind allegiance to the law, even when it is personally repressive. Joe's efforts to twist his homosexual desires into heterosexual form nearly destroy his wife Harper and shape him into the kind of man who is likely to succumb to the manipulations of a Roy Cohn. According to *Angels*, it is not Joe's homosexuality but rather his hypocritical and oppressive heterosexism that is morally reprehensible.

Although it is possible to understand and heal that kind of self-denial through self-examination, Kushner also warns that self-examination carries its own risks. This danger is especially pronounced when dogmatic faith has rendered a person susceptible to manipulation by charismatic deceivers, as is the case of Joe Pitt's allegiance to Roy Cohn. Such self-examination has also been popularized in both religious and secular groups. Apocalyptic groups in the United States and elsewhere give ample evidence of the easy slippage from being disciples of high-minded principles to becoming followers of vengeful and violent action against nonbelievers. David Koresh employed techniques of directed self-examination systematically to ensure the devotion of his followers. Far less extremist and tightly woven than the Branch Davidians are the numerous twelve-step programs that have been established throughout the United States. As different as they are in intent, what both kinds of groups have in common is their use of self-examination under the regulatory guidance of group-monitoring. *Angels* reminds us that it is worthwhile pondering the degree to which individual and group practices of self-examination extend or restrict personal agency and democratic citizenry.

In addition, through the character of Louis Ironson, *Angels* demonstrates that self-examination of an emotionally truncated self can result in little more than self-justification. Louis is given to such self-serving rationalizations, ironically through what appears to be a piercing interrogation of his motives. By overlaying abstract political issues onto his sense of self, he—like Roy Cohn—is able to countenance and even justify his personal abandonment of responsibility. In contrast to Cohn, who has no guilt about his actions, Louis is beset with guilt; indeed he has come to rely on it as a way of staving off commitment to others. His ostensible self-examination only aggravates a narcissism that diminishes his empathy for others.[8]

In striking contrast to the ostensibly upstanding yet morally injurious Joe Pitt and the emotionally immobilized Louis Ironson, *Angels'* most utopian character, the male nurse Belize, serves as a moral center in the play's whirlwind of immorality, amorality, and messianic righteousness. Kushner has conceded that making the only African American character in the play a nurse was "an inept thing to do," and I see his point.[9] But I would equally emphasize the value of depicting a strong male figure as a nurse, particularly one who makes what is clearly within the play's purview an illegal but ethical decision to steal the dead Roy Cohn's supply of AZT for Prior, who can't afford it. Earlier, in *Part One: Millennium Approaches*, when Prior teasingly expresses his gratitude to Belize for soothing his feverish body with "Magic goop" by declaring him "just a Christian martyr," Belize replies "Whatever happens, baby, I will be here for you."[10] With this sentiment, Kushner reauthorizes the Christian theme of brotherly love, extending it to gay men and to question the principle of capitalist profit-mongering for life-saving medicines. Belize accentuates an ethics of care as essential to men's integrity.

In the purview of the play, Prior Walter has been saved by the care he receives from Belize and learns to extend toward himself. At the conclusion of *Perestroika*, he is accompanied not only by Belize but also by his former lover Louis and Hannah Pitt, Joe Pitt's mother, each of whom have been morally transformed over the course of the drama. Indications are that Louis has shed some of his overweening self-involvement and that Hannah no longer adheres to the rigid moral system that had motivated her to try to "save" her son from homosexuality. By the time he speaks the final words of the play, "The Great Work Begins," Prior has—literally in the magical-realism sense—been to heaven and back. His decision to return to earth to seek "more life" constitutes what I mean by a skeptical revelation. He has unlearned the self-hatred of homophobia, which includes the view that AIDS is a justified death sentence. Characterizing himself as living with AIDS and committed to fostering full citizenship for himself and others who "won't die secret deaths anymore," he offers an alternative personal and social morality that resists the mandates of apocalyptic dogmatism.

I don't expect students necessarily to agree with all this. Nor should they be obliged to. The point of teaching on the threshold of revelation, is, after all, not to insist on some new dogma but to view all dogmas with skepticism. Moral education, if it means anything in a pluralistic society, surely means pondering the implications of competing moral systems. It means, as Margaret Walker has put it, gaining "confidence that our moral understandings and lifeways do not render us parochial, ethnocentric, domineering, or cruel with respect to others; that they do not leave us complicit in our own subjection, alienation, exploitation, and oppression; that the ways we live now are not simply empty, deluded, stupid, or pointless."[11]

Teaching on the threshold of revelation is a way of gaining such confidence and giving "more life" to thought. *Angels* is particularly exemplary in this respect because it challenges both the fatalistic view that nothing can be done to change the world and the relativistic view that the moral standing of a given act depends on the moral belief of the actor, regardless of consequence to others. It also wisely reminds us that

"Imagination is a dangerous thing."[12] Kushner's *Angels* thus cautions against the totalistic limits of dogmatic morality to make us more aware, as Toni Morrison has said in regard to the white-supremacist imagination that produces racism, "of the places where imagination sabotages itself, locks its own gates, pollutes its vision".[13] By carrying forth a blessing of more life, the skeptical classroom becomes a site of opportunity to imagine a different world, a place to reveal moral possibilities.

There was never any beginning or end,
but every day came before or after another
day. Every day did.
—*Gertrude Stein,* Ida

3 GENEALOGICAL SKEPTICISM: HOW THEORY CONFRONTS MILLENNIALISM

In the final years of the twentieth century, theory took some
heavy jabs from millennialists of all stripes. Disclosures about Paul de
Man's early writings and their links to the Third Reich were used to indict
virtually all French theory as collaborationist. At various times, both conservative and feminist pundits chastised theory for its arrogance. In this
chapter, I offer a defense of theory as necessary for combatting millennialism. Ironically, I may owe a debt to the attackers of theory since their
charges helped bring debates about theory to the attention of a larger
American audience. In addressing why theory is so valuable for that audience, I turn again to Tony Kushner's *Angels in America*, in particular *Perestroika*, for the way it explores the role of theory in our everyday lives.

Perestroika opens, like the Book of Genesis, with darkness and sound.
But rather than God's famous pronouncement, "Let there be light," here
we have a majestic voice from the darkness ushering in "Aleksii Antedil-
luvianovich Prelapsarianov, the World's Oldest Living Bolshevik." When
the light comes, what stands before us is, as the stage directions inform
us, a man "unimaginably old and totally blind." Staring out over the audience with unseeing eyes and in a voice resonant with age, Prelapsari-

anov utters words heard with greater frequency and growing intensity at the turn of the millennium: "The Great Question before us is: Are we doomed? The Great Question before us is: Will the Past release us? The Great Question before us is: Can we Change? In Time? And we all desire that Change will come." There is a brief pause and then these lines, delivered with "sudden violent passion": "And *Theory?* How are we to proceed without *Theory?* What system of Thought have these reformers to present to this mad swirling planetary disorganization, to the Inevident welter of fact, event, phenomenon, calamity? Do they have, as we did, a beautiful Theory, as bold, as Grand, as comprehensive a construct . . . ?"

Recalling the times when this "beautiful theory" enabled followers to view "in one all-knowing glance the mountainous, granite order of creation," Prelapsarianov expresses pity for the decline of the present day and scoffs at the current generation, the "Pygmy children of a gigantic race" who have only "market incentives," and "American cheeseburgers." Although he acknowledges the need to change, his final line is a warning that without a new "beautiful theory," "we dare not, we *cannot,* we MUST NOT move ahead!"[1]

Prelapsarianov's speech of longing, urgency, and need for omniscient truth and order should ring familiar to ears attuned to apocalypse and millennialism, whether religious or secular. Similarities in tone and content between apocalyptic belief and utopian Marxism have been noted before. But, as Kushner makes clear throughout Part Two of *Angels,* Prelapsarianov's words also aptly encapsulate the apocalyptic element in contemporary debates about theory and political change. This is the case not only for certain academic circles where theory bashing has become a popular theme but also among certain theoreticians who trudge onward in pursuit of metatheory. Like Prelapsarianov, both camps press forward in the name of change, which is, after all, hard to knock. Indeed, change carries the day in lots of creation stories. Genesis is certainly all about it: from darkness to light, from void to matter. And, in Christian tradition, Revelation is the story of the final change which brings the end of change. It is, nevertheless, possible to exhaust the energy of the idea of change. Indeed, we may have come pretty close to that in the United States through third-millennium-inspired rhetoric. Prelapsarianov's words, "we all desire that change will come," has been a refrain familiar to American ears since Bill Clinton's first presidential campaign; efforts to recharge that theme with metaphors of a bridge to the twenty-first century during his second campaign came off as tired by comparison, yet even more messianic in zeal.

One problem with any messianic stance toward change, as Kushner's characterization of Prelapsarianov suggests, is that it is blind to the very changes that are everywhere under way, changes that human actions have brought about and that we need to better understand. In contrast to meeting that need, the apocalyptic gaze sweeps with unseeing eyes over cultural continuities and discontinuities alike to evoke the one great change, a future of utopian promise, threatening that a false move will bring on its opposite, a tomorrow of hellish suffering. A far more pertinent view is the one captured in Gertrude Stein's sobering remark, "You can't change everything even if everything is changed."[2] Stein's observation is especially useful for clarifying the role of theory as explanation of social agency and change: it raises doubts about wholesale change yet leaves open possibilities of some sort of direction; it also acknowledges that enormous changes can occur through contingent circumstances that defy best or worst intentions.

Theory understood in this way is akin to what I mean by skeptical revelation, which seeks to reveal or describe accepted truths and normative judgments while striving to ascertain the ways that they came to be considered true. Such revelations are made through questioning the nature of truth, rather than believing in absolute Truth. In keeping with this stance, this chapter is a call for theory as a threshold place. Theory conceived in this way serves as both skeptical genealogy and what I discuss later as genealogical skepticism. Although these labels mean different things, in both cases, the point is neither to give up on theory nor to overload it, but to try to make a little sense of it and with it about how truths come to be constituted as such.

Disagreement about the status of truth is precisely why it does matter what we call a particular theory, not only because theory means so many different things to so many different people, but also because of the dismissal of theory as irrelevant or, worse, the denial of it as a form of truth-telling. Analysts from all over the political spectrum theorize, although they don't always label what they do as theory or seem to know they are theorizing. Over the past few decades, for example, apocalyptic urgency and millennialist promise have consolidated in the Religious Right's theory of governance. Christian Rightists like Ralph Reed and Jerry Falwell usually don't call their ideas theoretical, however, because they claim they are telling the divinely ordained, capital T, Truth. As a result, the mantle of theory tends to hang on the shoulders of secular thinkers; in academia, it is especially heavily draped around scholars of literature and culture. When taking up the mantle of theory, leftist circles have not always shied away from absolute Truth claims either. It is not too much of an exaggeration to say that I have encountered a few Prelapsarianovs of critical theory over the past decade. In fact, I have been a Prelapsarianov at times myself, which is why Kushner's stage direction specifying that Prelapsarianov be performed by a cross-dressed woman strikes me as particularly astute. Yet, in contrast to the intensifying dogmatic zeal of right-wing politics in the eighties and nineties, I would say that much of the left, and by this I mean radical theory and activism, has become more skeptical of millennialist pronouncements.

I regard this skepticism as the most important contribution of poststructuralist theory from the eighties. It is worth stressing how much poststructuralism has contributed because apocalyptic rhetoric so often surfaces in caricatures of poststructuralist theory penned by self-described antitheory critics. Apocalyptic allusions are used to narrate a story of theory's origin, its reign as a false messiah, and its imminent—and gladly awaited—fall. This use of apocalypticism confuses and complicates the notion of theory, or what is often tellingly called pure theory, with its odd but implied opposite, impure theory. Back in 1994, a *New York Times* article with the clever subtitle "Buddy, Can You Paradigm?" illustrated, albeit inadvertently, how apocalyptic views muddle these discussions. The article also serves as a historical marker for when the dismissal of theory went fully mainstream. Although the writer Ben Yagoda titled his article "Retooling Critical Theory," to suggest theory's continuation in another form, that view was undercut by his narrative of origin, end, and discipleship. Like numerous others, he pinpointed the 1966 Johns Hopkins conference as the "origin of theory's reign" where "French theorists like Jacques Derrida and Roland Barthes met their chief American disciples, [Paul] de Man and J. Hillis Miller."[3] As he put it, tongue in cheek, "a thousand theories bloomed." But the blooms of that day have since peaked and faded according to his article, the gist of which was to announce the "passing of theory."

Yagoda's report interested me not because it was so egregious but, rather, because it was and still is so typical of how apocalyptic structures interfere with conceptual differentiation by setting up an opposition between evil theory and good truth. I think this contributed to Yagoda's conflation of theory, deconstruction, and poststructuralism, all three of which were reductively cast as a common enemy. In keeping with apocalyptic narrative, he identified both the holy war that brought theory to its knees and a redemptive promise on the horizon. According to this version of history, the "resolution" of the culture wars gave theory its final blow. (The victory reportedly went to Camille Paglia, Dinesh D'souza, Roger Kimball, and David Lehman, who, if we follow the logic, serve as the four horsemen of theory's demise.) The millennialist hope was that their revelations of theory's obscurantist corruption would sufficiently humble theorists and prepare them for conversion experiences. Yagoda cited two possible paths. One was cultural studies, which he briefly described without much fanfare, leaving readers to wonder whether cultural studies proponents had indeed seen the light. In contrast, he trumpeted the "accessible, belletristic writing styles" of "such scholars as Henry Louis Gates, Frank Lentricchia, Alice Kaplan, Nancy Miller, Michael Berube, and Edward Said" who "have all made a transition from sometimes impenetrable high theory to prose, often explicitly autobiographical in cast, that is suitable—and intended for—comparatively wide audiences."[4]

The origin-and-end design of this rendition of theory not only propels us along a misleading timeline, it also presents a specious opposition between theory on one side and cultural studies and autobiography on the other. From this perspective, during the eighties, we suffered the penalty of Babel, otherwise known as theory, while the nineties allow us to rejoice in the epiphany of lucid cultural analysis and personal testimony. There are several problems with this formulation. For one thing, it is simply not the case that the writers cited earlier have suddenly and collectively been inspired to write intelligible prose. At least some of them already had a knack for it, even in the eighties. Furthermore, the other form of prose, that admittedly complex and often difficult form that antitheory buffs like to call the "unreadable" kind, has not exactly died out. However, it is more than ever drowned out by the chorus of complaints it receives within an academy and media touched by the effects of Rush Limbaugh's and Howard Stern's sound bite proclamations. Increasingly, technical vocabularies are depicted as fanatical plots and complexity a vice of the cultural elite.

Perhaps the most serious misunderstanding put forward in this account is that cultural criticism and autobiography intended for wider audiences are somehow precluded from theory. In this formulation, there is a tacit opposition between personal writings as truthful, and thus universally applicable, versus theory as devious and self-interestedly political. It is wrongly assumed that such writings reflect no insight from the theoretical accounts known as deconstruction and poststructuralism. I would say, in opposition to this view and to the equally mistaken apocalyptic portrayal of the end of theory, that such academic ventures as cultural studies and personal criticism are evidence not only of the value of poststructuralist theory but also, more crucially, of the continuing vigor and widening influence of its skepticism.

The emergence of the National Association of Scholars (N.A.S.) in the late eighties, along with similar groups like the Association of Literary Scholars and Critics (A.L.S.C.), which began in 1994, received significant media attention in the early nineties for attacking academics who regard theory as a valuable tool for analyzing literature and culture. Within both of these organizations, theory was often indicted as political correctness, a term which itself ranged considerably in meaning; depending on which political side was using it, to be "p.c." could either mean that one was politically progressive or dogmatically politicized. Over the decade since the founding of such groups, debates about political correctness have themselves pretty much come and gone. But these organizations, in particular the larger and better funded N.A.S., have retained a foothold in the academy. Membership has never been large—in 1997, the N.A.S. reported 4,000 and the A.L.S.C. 2,000 members. Despite small numerical representation, substantial funding by conservative groups like the Bradley, Heritage, and Olin Foundations have helped them publically promote their views.[5] On this front, what was called the "culture wars" did considerable damage to academic and public understandings of theory.

Given this skeptical genealogy of the theory question of the late twentieth century, what might a genealogical skeptic say and do about this state of affairs? Although conservative foundation funding already has and is likely to continue to offset the democratic potential of debate, the N.A.S. is best understood as a backlash to what *is*, in fact, a mainstreaming of politicized scholarship. Far from conceding to N.A.S. claims about either the nature or effect of such scholarship—I am contending that the politicization runs across the political spectrum and certainly includes the position of the N.A.S. Furthermore, the N.A.S. justifiably points out a consequential shift in the status of knowledge in our time. During the last quarter of the twentieth century, a number of cultural practices—theory being only one of the more explicit—made visible the ways in which truth, as William James said a century ago, happens to an idea. What poststructuralism added to James's insight was how power relations make truth happen to one idea over another. If that is indeed the case, then the least useful response to such organizations as the N.A.S. is to use the public arena to deny it. Genealogical skeptics are better served by using the N.A.S.'s well-funded publicity wedge to make it clear that this debate is politicized on all sides and is linked to issues of inadequate funding and less-than-democratic support of public education. Within that politicization, the greatest danger for the left as well as the right is to lay claim to absolute truth, and this is precisely where theory comes in. The question for me—which is not the great question as Prelapsarianov would have it, but rather a more modest question of a skeptic at work—is still this one: What can theory offer against apocalyptic zeal and millennialist assurances?

In the current debates about theory, it is important to reiterate that the forms of theory that most often get dismissed—those usually linked with the names Derrida and Foucault—are notable for their challenges to the beautiful theory for which Prelapsarianov awaits. There are at least two interrelated and misdirected antitheory responses to the Derridean and Foucauldian critiques. One is the put-down mentioned earlier that derides the difficult abstraction and opaque language of theory.

According to this argument, found in the academy and the mainstream press, theory is either a form of false consciousness or, worse yet, an attempt to humiliate the uninitiated. There is a flaw in logic here. Even if the payoff for wading through difficult prose does not prove worth the effort, it does not follow that theory is a conspiracy to establish a cadre of intellectual elites (even though it may be that for some). This attack on theory instates a specious opposition between truth as plain and simple and theory as complex and difficult.[6] Even though my experience suggests that some documents of proclaimed Truth are every bit as complex and difficult, not to mention unaccommodating, to deride it on that score strikes me as less a legitimate criticism than a symptom of anti-intellectualism.

Suffice it to say that sometimes theory is awfully difficult. The rationale would be that some modes of thought *are* hard-going. This is especially the case when it comes to what Foucault called "problemization," by which he meant taking ideas that seem perfectly natural and familiar to us and asking how they came to be so. This procedure is paramount for combatting dogmatism. In regard to combatting unnecessarily rarefied theory, a genealogically attuned response would do well to follow Gerald Graff's suggestion that we teach the conflicts.[7] From a skeptical perspective, this not only gives voice to competing theories (which at times Graff seems to suggest is sufficient), it encourages us also to make all theories and truth claims accountable, not on the basis of whether they are difficult but, rather, whether they are relevant, applicable, credible, and so forth.

A second antitheory claim, more often found in the academy (especially on the left) than in the mainstream press, takes skepticism about universals and moral absolutes so far as to arrive at the unfounded conclusion that theory is nothing more than tyranny through totalization.[8] According to this stance, theory is a tool of imperialistic hegemony. There is a certain irony about this charge, given the commendable efforts of poststructuralist theorists to dislodge totalization. I think the confusion arises from an overzealous rejection of theoretical generalization in favor of the local, particular, and specific.[9] In the name of difference, and sometimes invoking Foucault as the exemplary theorist of the local, we suffer the regime of the diminished plural. While adding "s" to key words like sexuality, theory, ethnicity, and so on, does help refute the standards of universality that uphold white supremacy, compulsory heterosexuality, and male privilege, even Foucault argued the necessity of grasping the wider context of local and particularized power relations. In other words, theorizing long-standing, deeply entrenched, culturally structured forces of injustice is not the same thing as providing globalized or teleological accounts. The dismissal or condemnation of theoretical scope has a pernicious effect, making us lose sight of overriding social relations that inhibit or prohibit practices of freedom, including the freedom to question the status quo.

As the discussion thus far indicates, to my mind the theoretical perspective that has been most vital for countering apocalyptic programs and universalist fallacies, whether on the right or the left of the political spectrum, is what Foucault—borrowing from Nietzsche—called genealogy. I single out Foucault's approach because his portrayals of the history of the present were explicitly, even though not always in practice, antiapocalyptic. His advocacy of genealogy was a way to challenge the search for an absolute origin, indicating that such a goal was really a metaphysical concept masquerading as history. The presumption that there is a single origin carries research in certain preordained directions which assume a continuity that crosses centuries unchanged, despite all the changes of culture that occur. The imposed coherence of origin-and-end thinking also ignores all the contingent effects that bring changes about in its single-minded pursuit of a single line of causality. In an effort to surmount this kind of history, Foucault proposed that historians should turn their attention to the ambiguous beginnings, contingencies, and incongruities of our existence.

Despite what antitheory arguments say about obfuscation, the Foucauldian notion of genealogy is not that much of a mystery. But it does give a jolt to some "tried and true" definitions, most profoundly to the traditional use of the term *genealogy* for establishing a family tree lineage. Take, for instance, the family tree outline found on the opening page of many editions of the Bible. The usual depiction is a graceful, symmetrical, harmonious and, quite literal, tree trunk and branches with blank spaces for names and dates. Every individual has the "right" number and gender designation for parents: two. Marriage and children are assumed in advance. It's all very neat and tidy. And that's precisely the contrast that Foucauldian genealogy makes clear. The actual facts for families—or trees—are often not neat, symmetrical, harmonious, socially sanctioned—or even known.

What genealogy insists on is that on both the personal and societal level, the family tree depiction of history often functions through systematic erasure and outright lies about the way people actually behave. Biological but "illegitimate" parentage, for example, is typically made invisible in favor of legally sanctioned paternity. Except for kings, queens, and presidents, partners of sexual affairs are rarely recorded. Same-sex intimacies go unnoted because of religious and secular laws and social norms that forbid or shun them. And in U.S. history, official family tree lineages helped conceal the rape and impregnation of enslaved women by their white masters. Genealogical investigation seeks to discover precisely these kinds of erasures that have to be written back in in order to understand and reconfigure the history of the present. Discovering the traces of such sexual and racial counter-memories are the means by which genealogy establishes a historical knowledge of social life. In *Power/Knowledge* Foucault offers a succinct statement of genealogy's make-up and political purpose: "Let us give the term *genealogy* to the union of erudite knowledge and local memories which allows us to establish a historical knowledge of struggles and to make use of this knowledge tactically today."[10]

The Foucauldian notion of genealogy provides a base for the pursuit of skeptical revelation, but I also want to emphasize some important extensions of and departures from that conceptualization. Foucault was never explicit about just what constitutes erudite knowledge. Consequently, his writings have received deserved criticism for their inadequate attention to gender and race. Furthermore, some of his efforts to differentiate genealogy from Marxism on the one hand, and deconstruction on the other, confuse more than clarify the status of truth as a production of power/knowledge. But feminist, queer, and critical race theories have provided a number of crucial correctives. As a method, genealogy gains perceptive leverage through the analytical tools of Marxist analysis and deconstruction. Genealogy has also been enhanced by literary studies, especially through the strategies of oppositional reading that groups like the A.L.S.C. are so worried about. In turn, each of these critical approaches benefits from a genealogical focus; otherwise they risk totalizing truth by too steadfastly relying on abstraction, self-reference, and conceptual coherence. This is the case, for example, when feminism analyzes gender as a category separate and distinct from race, class, and sexuality. Or when deconstruction too facilely relies on its axiom of binary oppositions as "always already" there; that too is a pitch for origin, albeit disguised.

An ongoing skeptical use of Foucault's ideas—in other words both a skeptical genealogy and a genealogical skepticism—necessitates evaluating these reorientations of knowledge. Skepticism grounded by genealogy recognizes that knowledge is always partial in both senses of the word: it is necessarily fragmentary and imbued with one's own well-being and affiliations in mind. Because it is finite, it is crucial to be as thorough as possible. And because it can never be completely impartial, it is crucial for analysts to discern the other side of the threshold, so to speak, that which motivates purveyors of other knowledge. By such means we entitle ourselves to speak the truth as we have come to know it even as we acknowledge that other people's truths will be different, often to the point of conflict.

A skeptical view of truth as contested thus makes no claims for universality. But it is important to attend to how this argument is made in various contexts. These days, challenges to claims of universality are hardly new. Once found pretty exclusively as a radical leftist position, this view has been taken up by mainstream segments in the United States. For example, multiculturalism, formerly isolated in college and university curricula, or distinguishable as a rallying cry for radical democracy, has become a public relations strategy for multinational corporations. This is not to say that assumptions of universality, teleology, and progress have been entirely cast off. On the contrary, they have been readorned through new articulations. The task of skeptical genealogy is to reveal and analyze the power dynamics of these intricately patterned masks of dominant power/knowledge. Such unmasking is not the same as renouncing since it is quite possible for certain translations of universality in the name of difference to promote, perhaps inadvertently, new forms of subjectivity that foster equality. Being able to discern differing consequences is integral to skeptical inquiry.

Thus far I have been discussing theory largely as it is undertaken within the field known as cultural studies. As I indicated earlier, I see the turn toward personal criticism on the part of many academics these days also as enhancing theory, rather than replacing it as Yagoda argued. By grounding the abstraction of theory in self-narrative, personal criticism, as Nancy Miller argues, "opens an inquiry on the cost of writing."[11] Miller makes a cogent case for why personal criticism is not divorced from theory, showing how the tension between the personal and the positional enliven theoretical reflection; in other words, she employs a form of personalized genealogy that reflects skeptically on the links between truth and writing. Following from that perspective, I want to show how certain works of literature enhance theory through genealogical skepticism. As I have indicated, *Angels in America* is one such work, but I want to turn first to a novel that boldly enacts genealogical skepticism, Toni Morrison's *Jazz*, from 1992.

Using terms like *genealogy* and *skepticism* to describe Morrison's novel is a way of marking its break with the two other strands of literary tradition most often drawn on in critical responses to *Jazz*: historical and postmodern fiction. Rather than either of these designations, I would call *Jazz* a work of genealogical fiction. One reason to make this distinction is to address some of the negative criticisms that the novel received upon publication from a number of reviewers who either disparaged it for unconvincing character motivation or dismissed it as pretentiously postmodern. Such criticisms either assume or promote a goal of historical realism and then lay blame on Morrison for not living up to their definition of good fiction. This is the thrust of David Mason's comments when he states that his impression "on finishing Toni Morrison's latest historical fiction was that here was a short story inflated by literary style." He echoes the sentiment expressed by several mainstream literary reviewers when he goes on to say that "Morrison's narrator is merely an anonymous literary presence who has studied postmodernism."[12]

Mason's reading, which ties in with antitheory sentiment, seems to me equally off the mark in its understanding of postmodernism. The narrative voice of *Jazz* does, I believe, reflect postmodernist thought, but it also incorporates the genealogical dimension of postmodernism, which assiduously studies the past, acknowledges its inconsistencies, and speculates on the consequences of everyday events—the matter of history—on the lives of those in the present. In *Jazz*, the narrator's disposition toward the past and present enacts a defining trait of what I mean by genealogical skepticism. Genealogical fiction focuses on history but does not adhere to the teleological assumptions and unifying narrative conventions of a historical novel. And even though genealogical fiction may employ postmodernist techniques in order to break with the narrative coherence of conventional historical fiction, it does not promulgate a postmodernist sense of crisis.

In its performance of the history of the present, genealogical fiction—or poetry or drama—breaks the hold of official truth and the metaphysics of memory, putting in their place the truths of countermemory. *Jazz* is an exemplar of this type of literature because its story of beginnings reopens a door barred by the concealments of the official, white-supremacist narrative of the past. The question of genealogy as a study of the descent of family and historical lines is one of the problematics on which *Jazz* specifically focuses.[13] The novel is filled with characters whose family lines are like a skein of tangled thread, with mothers and fathers who have been taken from their children or whose identities remain mysterious. There is the self-named character Joe Trace, who searches for his mother and seeks a sign that she is the woman Wild, whose own name reveals not her lineage but her existence. Hunter's admonition to Joe that Wild is "*somebody's* mother and *somebody* ought to take care" holds in it an ethical imperative not entirely dependent on traditional family obligation. The story and name of Golden Gray, the son of the "white lady" Vera Louise Gray and "a Negro boy from out Vienna way" is the kind of subjugated truth that dispels the deceptions recorded in the "family tree" histories of white slaveowners.[14] The story of Dorcas, whose parents were brutally killed in the riots of 1926 when whites in East St. Louis murdered over 200 blacks, branches into the story of Violet Trace, herself the daughter of a mother who committed suicide. Ironically, perhaps inexplicably, Violet's obsession with Dorcas, whose corpse she tries to disfigure after Dorcas has been killed by Joe, turns from hatred to devotion and enables them to love each other again.

The intertwined lives of these and so many others become Morrison's genealogy of the city itself, which, like jazz, tantalizes with its call and response, syncopations, improvisations, and sudden spirals from joy to sorrow and back again. As the narrator explains, telling about human existence must entail "something rogue. Something else you have to figure in before you can figure it out."[15] This something rogue is what distinguishes skeptical genealogy from both traditional history and apocalyptic theory. By dramatizing the rogue events, people, and places that are excised from conventional history, *Jazz* refutes the founding tenets of millennialist thought: the tracing of origin as the singular, miraculous moment from which all meaning and privilege derive; the insistence on continuity and influence, from origin to end; the disavowal of contingency, accident, and novelty in the dispersion of events that have impact on our lives; and the electist claim to possess *the* beautiful theory as a guide toward a reign of peace and harmony. *Jazz* challenges the modes of knowledge that have invented the past in such a way as to justify current injustices and cruelties as ordained or inevitable and to lay claim on the future.

As a work like *Jazz* illustrates, the value of genealogical literature for theorizing the history of the present resides in its powerful effect: the truth that it induces into our present reality. Giving pride of place to the literary in this way has historical, philosophical, and political rationales. As Evan Simpson and Mark Williams have argued, "the ability to read fiction is itself a considerable achievement" of modern culture. Pointing out that understanding operative truths *as fiction*, which allows us to evaluate them on the basis of aesthetic categories such as "coherence, complexity, and comprehensiveness," they argue further, following Wittgenstein, that "justification comes to an end in judgments that hold fast."[16] What skeptical genealogy adds to this is the persistent evaluation of that which does "hold fast."

Genealogical skepticism also encourages us to become storytellers who are conscientious truth-makers. As Foucault observed, it is possible "to make fiction work within truth, to induce truth-effects within a fictional discourse, and in some way to make the discourse of truth arouse, 'fabricate' something which does not yet exist, thus 'fiction' something. One 'fictions' history starting from the political reality that renders it true, one 'fictions' a politics that doesn't yet exist starting from an historical truth."[17]

In *The Order of Things* Foucault demonstrated how this fictioning occurred in the historical emergence of new categories of thought, such as the human sciences, which over the past century came to be seen as a natural truth yet have now undergone their own crises of status. To use the United States as another example, we might think here of Garry Wills's persuasive argument about how Thomas Jefferson and others "invented America" in their fictioned politics known as the Declaration of Independence.[18]

Just what new form of politics might emerge from the ways genealogical skeptics think about truth and change remains to be seen, but *Angels in America* provides some glimpses of how genealogical dramatizations might work "within truth." Foremost among these fictionings is the role that friendship plays in *Angels* to foster new truths to live by. The truth effect of friendship as an art of life comes full-force in the final scene of *Perestroika*. Gathered at the fountain four years later, the company of friends would be by many standards of judgment an unlikely assortment: a gay man with AIDS, a Mormon woman, a black male nurse, a gay Jewish intellectual. Any such characterization would be equally inadequate, since their identities are neither fixed nor monolithic. Their lives have distinct past experiences, dissimilar beliefs, and different trajectories. Yet together they have cultivated their differences in identity and health and outlook in order to forge a friendship that elevates each.

The nature of their new friendship is encapsulated in a dialogical revelation about the role of theory. Louis, the member of the group who has been most linked to unified theoretical abstraction, begins the exchange by pointing to the effects of Perestroika: "It's all too much to be encompassed by a single theory now." Hannah offers her own view of the complexity between theorizing and living: "You can't live in the world without an idea of the world, but it's living that makes the ideas. You can't wait for a theory, but you have to have a theory." And Louis replies, "Go know. As my grandma would say." Together they then relate the story of the angel Bethesda, each one bringing his or her own special interest into the telling, Louis emphasizing history, Belize healing, Hannah spiritual redemption. In this last scene, Prior is the one who orchestrates the collective telling, and thus becomes the artist-friend who makes the final pronouncement that the "Great Work Begins."

By the conclusion of *Perestroika*, then, the "beautiful theory" that Prelapsarianov espoused without equivocation at the outset has been replaced by a declaration for the start of "Great Work" which will foster "*More Life.*" Some critics have found this final scene too saccharine, a fall from radical grace. But I think this misses the point of how the fictioning of new politics can come about. At any rate, I personally find Kushner's effort to make a fictional link between friendship and citizenship enticing. On this view, the blessing of "*More Life*" serves as a defining characteristic of a new politics of friendship which calls not only for citizens to be friends but also, more adventurously, for friends to be citizens. Citizens as friends, of course, is not a new concept. Its lineage goes back to ancient Greece and reemerged in the neoclassical era. But such friendship was for an elite company of men, who could allow a fostering of emotional bonds within their privileged sphere of decision making. More than two millennia later, Kushner is extending the scope of the idea of citizens as friends as a way of embracing a greater diversity of citizens. He also emphasizes what is increasingly, in these days of privatization of so many facets of our lives, its necessary correlary: friends as citizens.

At this point it *is* too fanciful to think that the United States could become a nation of friendly citizens. Too many of the hierarchical conditions of capitalism and entrenched racism and sexism prevail. However, the notion of friends aspiring toward full citizenship for themselves and each other carries an aspiration that is worth deliberating about. Will citizen-friends be able to salvage democracy in the third millennium? Skeptical theory does not even try to make that kind of millennialist prophecy. But it does suggest that the effort to revalue democracy in this way is worth a try.

I desire that there may be as many different
persons in the world as possible.
—*Henry D. Thoreau,* Walden

Axiom 1: People are different from each other.
—*Eve Kosofsky Sedgwick,* Epistemology of the Closet

4 MILLENNIALIST MORALITY AND THE PROBLEM OF CHASTITY

Chastity is breaking out all over. The new abstinence movement has been around for a while now, but lately it has been bolstered
by millennialist dreams of a transcendent or bodiless body. It first came
to my attention on daytime television talk shows. Before Phil Donahue
left the air, one of his shows in 1994 featured several men and women
enthusiastically endorsing a "full way of life without sexuality."[1] A large
banner behind the guest lineup proclaimed one of the slogans that the
Southern Baptist Convention places on billboards and buses: "'VIR-
GIN': Teach your kids it's not a dirty word." The panel on this day included three white college students who spoke at campuses around the
country on behalf of a program called "True Love Waits." Waiting means
premarital sexual abstinence—including a strict ban on masturbation.
Two of these young adults testified that their own five-year celibate relationship would not have been possible without their commitment to
God. But they generously indicated that, for those who haven't been
waiting, there is always "secondary virginity," a second chance for sexual
purity. What people should do in either case, they advised, is take the official pledge, often recited at a proto-wedding event: "Believing that true
love waits, I make a commitment to God, myself, my family, those I date,

my future mate, and my future children to be sexually pure until I enter a covenant marriage relationship."

Is Chastity White? The Straight Story

It's not easy to make chastity hip for the current generation of adolescents, 55 percent of whom are sexually active by the time they are seniors in high school.[2] One approach that seems to be having some success is to make chastity a multicultural event. Donahue's two other guests were African American men, A. C. Green, NBA basketball player for the Phoenix Suns, and Mike Hill, member of the religious rap group ETW (End Time Warriors). Green is a founding member of "Athletes for Abstinence," a group which advocates virginity as a commitment until marriage. Hill, who argues that condoms encourage premarital sex, showed a clip of his music video in which he raps against safe sex campaigns. On that day, a caller who identified himself as a black gay man revealed that he too practiced abstinence, but that in his case, there was no commitment to God. His sexual abstinence, he admitted, stemmed from fear of AIDS. The guests offered no response. Untypically, neither did Donahue. A momentary silence ensued and then Donahue was off to work the audience.

The Donahue show may have gone by the wayside, but certain of its features help pinpoint ongoing contradictions within a popular appropriation of multiculturalism. One of these is between race and sexual difference. As the playout of the television show example indicates in regard to chastity, race difference was deemed acceptable but sexual difference was not. The electist rationale behind this was clear enough from watching the show: chastity was seen as the prerogative of heterosexual believers because they alone—regardless of racial or ethnic lineage— could celebrate the joy of premarital abstinence and eventually enjoy marital, procreative sexuality. From this perspective, an abstaining homosexual was simply refraining from an "unnatural act." If multiculturalism is to have any meaning beyond the superficial, it must provide a clearer understanding of the ways in which our everyday lives have been differentially informed by sexual preference, race, ethnicity, class, and gender.[3] As both the strengths and the shortcomings of the Donahue show demonstrate, issues of sexuality are much more central to this effort than has generally been recognized.

With apocalyptic fear and millennialist righteousness fueling Christian Right fervor, the already entrenched polarization between advocates of sexual freedom and proponents of sexual restraint has steadily grown more pronounced, to the point of becoming programmatic. In 1996, federal legislation entitling abstinence-based programs to half a billion dollars over a five-year period further polarized the terms of the discussion—and ensured that chastity would have a monolithic meaning at the outset of the twenty-first century.[4] In order to be eligible for the funds, within a year, 1,500 to 2,400 schools across the nation had adopted the two leading abstinence-only curricula, "Sex Respect" and "Teen Aid."[5] Claimed as a moral victory by the Christian Right, these programs divide sexual education and sexuality into two incommensurable camps, those who support abstinence until marriage and those who don't. A variety of names attach to each one—the sinners versus the saints, the decent versus the indecent, the moral versus the immoral—but the stance is clear: chastity means abstinence for heterosexual, monogamous, marriage-bound youth.

Genealogical skepticism might help in altering the terms of that polarization by setting the current debate about chastity within the context of various movements for sexual freedom and restriction that have been a vital but often-ignored component of U.S. society.[6] Such an approach calls for literary as well as historical attention, precisely because genealogy establishes the extent to which these two fields of knowledge intertwine to create the kind of "politics of truth" discussed in the previous chapter. On this view, literature does not merely provide a window on historical truth—it helps materialize it. Conversely, as literary analysis conducted with genealogical scrutiny indicates, social movements are often the nub of literary drama, and this is especially the case in regard to sexuality.

A closer look at some of the discourses of chastity and sexuality from the past century and a half, both literary and historical, helps differentiate between the dogmatically normative forms of morality and skeptically inclined nonnormative forms. Some espousals of chastity are stridently disciplinary, for instance, as was the case with Sylvester Graham's

Lecture to Young Men on Chastity (1834). This is also the case with "True Love Waits." The goal of such efforts is to regulate groups, often whole populations, toward a single standard of moral conduct codified as "normal." The view of normality that is being put forward is infused with apocalyptic notions of sexuality and bodies as sinful and millennialist longings for freedom from flesh.

But there are other ways to think about bodies, sexuality, and chastity, such as Thoreau's chapter on "Higher Laws" in *Walden*, which is also moral or ethical in goal but nonregulatory in training and orientation. Rather than striving toward moral conformity around a homogenous definition of normality, such nondisciplinary discourses encourage individualized expressions of chastity. They comprise what Foucault called an aesthetic ethics.[7] As a way of demonstrating the important distinctions between these disciplinary code-oriented and nondisciplinary modes of morality, I first highlight the range and recurrency of the problem of chastity in U.S. culture and then offer an analysis of the wedding gift that Thoreau sent to his friend and long-time correspondent H. G. O. Blake, the "disconnected fragment" that he called "Chastity and Sensuality." In light of apocalyptic pressure toward conformity, Thoreau's essay is a "gift that keeps on giving," to use the lingo of postmodern advertising. Its skepticism toward the requirements of compulsory heterosexuality and narrow definitions of chastity are still vital today.

R-E-S-P-E-C-T: Give It to Me, Give It to Me, Give It to Me

Chastity movements in the United States, of course, are hardly new. As historians of sexuality and gender have shown, the promotion of chastity has a long history in this nation, a history intertwined with movements for sexual freedom. At various times, perhaps first most notably in the 1830s and 1840s, chastity advocates have attained impressive followings. Sylvester Graham filled large lecture halls and had thousands of readers eager to try the Graham System of restricted diet and sexuality. Grahamite boarding houses devoted to his principles sprung up around the country.[8] And at the turn of the century up through the First

World War, purity crusaders were joined by medical reformers and legislators in an effort to control the spread of venereal disease. The social hygiene movement emphasized chastity for men and women and directed much of its energy against prostitution.[9]

What is unprecedented for the United States, however, is the extent to which the view of the Religious Right has come to permeate discussions of sexuality. Consider the following "analysis" from a 1992 editorial in the *Wall Street Journal:*

> Last year Americans learned that Magic Johnson had contracted the AIDS virus, New York City schools were handing out condoms to adolescents, and a nephew of President John F. Kennedy had had sex with a woman he picked up in a bar. Each news event was about something altogether alien to contemporary culture: sin.
>
> Sin isn't something many people spent much time worrying about in the past 25 years. But we will say this for sin: it at least offered a frame of reference for behavior. When the frame was dismantled during the sexual revolution, we lost the guidewire of personal responsibility, the rules for proper conduct of sexual relations.[10]

When contrary views are expressed, the Religious Right has waged and won some powerful battles. Take the case of *Sassy*, a magazine geared to a teenage audience. When *Sassy* instituted a sex education column with specific information about masturbation, orgasm, homosexuality, pregnancy, and so on, a group called Women Aglow worked through a Jerry Falwell–supported publication called *Focus on the Family* to launch a campaign against the column. By writing to *Sassy*'s advertisers and threatening to boycott their products, they managed to get substantial reduction in the magazine's advertising account. *Sassy* removed the column.[11]

More directly assaultive of the constitutional commitment to separation of church and state, and thus to democratic freedom, is the entrenchment of Christian fundamentalist values in public schools, specifically in sexual education programs. The single most evident victory for these theocratic forces is the formal adoption of their sex education curriculum known as "Sex Respect." By 1994, one in four U.S. public school districts were teaching this or its related version "Teen-Aid."[12] This sweep of "family-life" legislation is part of a concerted effort by the

Christian Right to bring about Bible-based social reform by working outward from the grassroots, local school board level. The Christian Coalition has been hugely successful for several reasons. The campaign itself has benefited from its polarized focus on chastity versus sexual decadence, the determination and energetic work of its supporters, and large government subsidies from the Reagan, Bush, and Clinton administrations.[13] The backdrop of rising AIDS incidence in adolescents provides Sex Respect supporters with a quotient of fear that feeds into the apocalypticism of fundamentalist belief.

The Christian Right's pitch for "family values" is a theocratic assault on democratic values.[14] In the case of Sex Respect, the threat of church-based government is compounded by informational omissions, misrepresentations and inaccuracies. The Sex Respect curriculum fails to provide a discussion of the effectiveness of birth control methods other than complete abstinence. Discussions of abortion exclusively use anti-choice language, referring to it as a decision to "kill the baby."[15] Teen-Aid insists that "the only way to avoid pregnancy is to abstain from genital contact" and further indicates that even the correct use of condoms will not prevent HIV infection.[16] In the face of rising AIDS incidence and pregnancy among adolescents, such inadequate and biased teaching is insidious. It is necessary to insist on sexual education programs that do provide sufficient information to students so that they can indeed make decisions about their sexuality. This does, of course, include information about abstinence. As it stands now, however, the Religious Right has a headlock on chastity.

But there is more than one way to think about chastity. Nineteenth-century Grahamism was in many ways the historical counterpart to the Religious Right's emphasis on sexual self-control, sexually transmitted disease, and the decline of family values. In both cases, the advocacy of chastity emerged as part of a backlash against movements for sexual freedom. In Graham's era, the "threat" was from freethinkers like Fanny Wright who sought in particular to strengthen women's sexual freedom. In this era, the Religious Right is committed to overturning gains made by feminism and the gay and lesbian movement. Despite these similarities, Graham's motivation was not religious fundamentalism. In helping to define the New Chastity Movement, he stressed physiological principles of health rather than divine decree as the sole rationale for sexual self-control. Grahamism's dread of disease and debility is clearly manifest in the list of effects he indicated were the result of sexual excess:

languor, lassitude, muscular relaxation, general debility and heaviness, depression of spirits, loss of appetite, indigestion, faintness and sinking at the pit of the stomach, increased susceptibilities of the skin and lungs to all the atmospheric changes, feebleness of circulation, chilliness, headache, melancholy, hypochondria, hysterics, feebleness of all the senses, impaired vision, loss of sight, weakness of the lungs, nervous cough, pulmonary consumption, disorders of the liver and kidneys, urinary difficulties, disorders of the genital organs, spinal diseases, weakness of the brain, loss of memory, epilepsy, insanity, apoplexy[17]

Whereas for Graham, these symptoms were auto-induced and today's concern is largely focused on transmission between sexual partners, his insistence on the relationship between sexual excitation and disease resembles contemporary anxiety-based abstinence programs, secular as well as religious. Fear of AIDS and other sexually transmitted diseases is fueled by similar warnings of dire physical symptoms; images of bodily deterioration are used as evidence of a justified punishment. Generating fear in this way readily translates into fear and hatred of people with AIDS.

As feminist historians such as Linda Gordon, Nancy Cott, and Carroll Smith-Rosenberg have shown, nineteenth-century middle-class women found that chastity movements often enhanced their power in regard to birth control. Although it was not exclusively so, this motivation for chastity was frequently secular in orientation, emphasizing the value of a small family for economic and emotional security. In terms of gender history, one of the key elements in chastity movements is the importance placed on men's responsibility for their own sexuality. Seen in light of chastity movements, the sexual revolution of the 1960s and 1970s was a setback because it placed the onus of responsibility for birth control almost exclusively on women, regardless of their marital status. Like the earlier chastity movement, the current one returns to a focus on male responsibility. Even with greater accessibility to contraception, many of today's college-aged virgins, male and female, report that, in addition to wanting a committed relationship and fearing AIDS, their foremost reason for practicing abstinence is unwanted pregnancy.[18]

In an entirely secular vein, Julia Phillips cites a combination of reasons for what might be called virtual chastity for herself and others in Hollywood: a yuppie work ethic that saps energy, disenchantment with potential partners, distaste for condoms, fear of sexually transmitted diseases, and a new emphasis on sobriety.[19] And then there is the postmodern promotion of chastity for style's sake, as with an ad from the *Village Voice* that announces "Quality Leather *Chastity Belts* now available in a variety of colors reflecting the trend of the 90s. More than 15 exclusive styles with working locks and keys created to be worn over clothing from men and women." The ad's photo image is of two young women playing pool. Their tight jeans are enhanced with crotch-covering chastity belts that would make Michael Jackson proud. The top of the ad proclaims: "Redefine the New Sexual Revolution."

Chastity and religion do, of course, often go hand in hand, but the diversity of religious teachings about sexual abstinence and activity is extensive. The Shakers are well-known for their strict prohibition on any form of sexuality, making abstinence a lifetime commitment even for married partners, but their beliefs differ notably from the vows of life-long celibacy that Catholic priests and nuns take. No Shaker worth his or her salt would espouse the view expressed in "Chastity as Shared Strength: An Open Letter to Students," written by the director of counseling services at Alvernia, a Franciscan College; she defines chastity as a *temporary, non-genital* commitment to this three-fold love of God, others, and ourselves" (emphasis hers).[20] On this view, genital commitment is a requirement of marriage. Within the African American community, Afro-centricity has contributed to changing sexual practices. In "Young, Hot and Celibate," Veronica Chambers explains that a number of her friends are making commitments to the Nation of Islam's principle of pre-marital abstinence in order "to rise to higher levels, spiritually and mentally."[21]

Even with this brief overview, it is clear that there are many different ways to think about and practice chastity. Attention to this diversity helps problematize the monolithic and monopolistic sexual views promulgated by the Religious Right. Amidst this diversity, Henry David

Thoreau provides one of the most intriguing approaches to chastity. By situating his ideas within nineteenth-century debates over sexuality, marriage, and reproduction, I want to show the ways in which Thoreau's espousal of chastity challenged the heteronormative electism of his time. He presents chastity as a mode of moral conduct that is skeptical of mandates to regulate sexuality. Next, by recontextualizing his discussion of sexual morality within current debates in literary studies, I want to illuminate the limits of heteronormative assumptions in contemporary critical analysis, not just in regard to Thoreau, but in general. Here I seek to emphasize that desire is different for different people. Put concisely, reading through the lens of normative sexuality constrains the way we read. It places a cataract over desire's intricate possibilities.

Epistemology of a Transcendental Closet

"Chastity and Sensuality" was the second of two "fragments" that Thoreau sent to his friend H. G. O. Blake. The first is titled "Love" and both were enclosed in a brief letter addressed to "Mr. Blake." The first paragraph simply explains the enclosure: "Here come the sentences which I promised you. You may keep them if you will & use them as the disconnected fragments of what I may find to be a complete essay, on looking over my journal at last, and may claim again." The second short paragraph completes the letter: "I send you the thoughts on chastity & sensuality with diffidence and shame, not knowing how far I speak to the condition of men generally, or how far I betray my peculiar defects. Pray enlighten me on this point if you can." It is signed "Henry D. Thoreau."[22] Thoreau himself never converted these pieces to formal essays (although they are generally referred to as essays), but they were published after his death in F. B. Sanborn's edition of Thoreau's *Familiar Letters*.

When critics specifically comment on "Chastity and Sensuality," it is often in a tone of slight embarrassment over his "conventional, Victorian sense of sexual morality."[23] Charles Anderson calls it a "curious example of Victorian prudery, a steady evasion of sex."[24] Some take his disclosure of "shame" and the suggestion of "peculiar defects" as an admission of intense sexual anxiety coupled with a disdainful attitude toward women, as typified by Richard Bridgman's remark that "Thoreau could think abstractly of marriage when it was removed from the tiresomeness of women and the grossness of the sexual connection."[25] James Armstrong, also assuming strong sexual fear, associates that fear with a fear of tuberculosis and his susceptibility to bronchitis. Armstrong demonstrates the links between Grahamism and other physiologically inspired social reformers of the day, arguing that "the basic motive for Thoreau's asceticism, both dietary and sexual, was his desire to reduce the threats to his uncertain health that the reformers maintained were offered by gastric and genital excitement."[26] Richard Lebeaux offers "fear of death" as a key to Thoreau's equations between sexuality and the "bodily and animal nature of the self."[27] In short, these brief discussions of "Chastity and Sensuality" interpret it as symptomatic of Thoreau's sexual anxieties or inadequacies.

This interpretation carries over to discussions of his sexuality in general, in which he is recurrently characterized as sexually ambivalent.[28] This is not to say that there has been consensus about Thoreau's sexuality, since critics have variously designated him as asexual, heterosexual, or homosexual, but, rather, that there has been consistency in seeing his writing *as symptomatic* of fear of sex. If seen as primarily heterosexual, he is seen as weakly so. If asexual, it is because of his intense narcissism. If homosexual, it is said to be unconscious or latent.

In a review of this debate about Thoreau's sexuality, Walter Harding concludes that Thoreau "was not without a sexual drive," his "heterosexual drive was low, indeed almost non-existent," and "both his actions and words, consciously and/or subconsciously, indicate a specific sexual interest in members of his own sex." Adding that there is no "concrete evidence" of homosexual activity on Thoreau's part, he also points out that it is "perfectly possible, of course, for him to have had a few homosexual incidents without our finding any evidence of it."[29] Although Harding puts far less emphasis on anxiety and fear, the value he places on Thoreau's ability to sublimate has the effect of applauding a nonsexual existence. As numerous other critics do, he draws on Freud's theory of sublimation, citing Thoreau's devotion to nature and his achievement of literary mastery as the "outlet for all Thoreau's sexual energy," adding that the "thwarting of his desires backfired into his genius."[30]

To my mind, the most significant information that Harding provides is relegated to a footnote in which he states that there was "a homosexual scandal in Concord involving a number of Thoreau's contemporaries which resulted in some of the participants being driven from town. So even despite Victorian reticence such activities were not left unreported."[31] In the text of his essay, Harding argues that any homosexual activity on Thoreau's part, at least with any frequency, would most likely have been similarly discovered and reported. Harding passes too quickly over the implications of this so-called "homosexual scandal," which might more aptly be called a homosexual purge. Although the particular incident to which he refers occurred around the time of Thoreau's death and hence would have no bearing on his writings, the way the townspeople reacted is a register of their attitude toward male-male sexuality, an oppressiveness consonant with Massachusett's antisodomy laws.

I recount these studies here because I think they are themselves symptomatic—not of sexual anxiety per se, but of a culturally constituted anxiety that seeks relief by ordering and categorizing sexual desire and gauging it according to a standard of normality. In this regard, they provide a pattern of scholarship geared around what Foucault described as a deployment of sexuality, a "great chase after the truth of sex, the truth in sex" through which our bodies are medicalized in the name of the body politic, socialized into procreative behavior, and our pleasures, if judged unmanageable, are labeled perverse and then corrected.[32] The important point for my discussion is that this deployment functions as a disciplinary mode, which operates by categorizing people according to sexual identity. The categories themselves are instrumental in the process of normalization and discipline because they divide along lines of the normal versus abnormal, acceptable versus unacceptable, legal versus illegal. To the extent that our scholarly endeavors follow this line of investigation and its reductive assignments of sexual identity, they consolidate the deployment of sexuality within the discipline of literary criticism. Accepting heterosexuality and marriage as normative pathologizes other expressions of desire as symptomatically asexual or homosexual or simply perverse; even if unintended, such a view bolsters disciplinary educational programs such as Sex Respect.

Freud's theory of sublimation as an accounting for artistic "genius" is part of this deployment.[33] It is trapped in a logic that first condemns homosexuality as a pathology and then condones its expression only in aesthetic form. Although I have no doubt that critics mean well when they praise Thoreau's powers of sublimation, it is no discredit to Thoreau's prose to say that the suppression of his desire is more likely to have thwarted his literary expression. For what is everywhere visible in his prose is a combination of sexual longing, joy, and suppression. Jonathan Katz is a notable exception among critics in his documentation of the ways in which Thoreau's writings range between unambiguous expressions of male-male desire and love and secretive descriptions in which the gender of a loved friend is rendered ambiguous or elided.[34] As Katz suggests, Thoreau's writing is more closeted than sublimated. Given the social and legal opposition to male-male desire and sexuality, this is hardly surprising; it should help us see that the sense of fear that critics detect in Thoreau's discussions about sexuality is more likely a fear of social disgrace and punishment of the kind meted out to his contemporaries when they were driven from Concord.

None of the mentioned normative views do any justice to the intricacies of Thoreau's discussion of sexuality and chastity. Eve Sedgwick's groundbreaking theorization of queer desire provides a more perceptive approach. Sedgwick has enabled us to see how the literary closet reframes and transvalues desires so that they might see the light of day. Sedgwick's insights make clear the shortcomings of normative systems of knowledge. This has surely been the case with Thoreau criticism. Thoreau's journals, letters, and published works are laced through with desire, desire that defies any simple classification. In many and various ways, he describes the thrill of seeing men's bodies, adoration for women like Lidian Emerson, bittersweet desire for "a gentle boy" like Edmund Sewell, and a sensuous delight in nature. Precisely because of these diverse expressions of desire and love, reading Thoreau through the constraints of prelabeled sexual classification systems limits our understanding of his ideas and his aesthetic principles. More crucially, this deployment of normative and normalizing reading perpetuates the very system of discipline that Thoreau's writings so often challenge.

In specific regard to "Chastity and Sensuality," the predominant critical view has missed Thoreau's critique of normative heterosexuality as mere sensuality, devoid of spirituality. Indeed, it has missed the major formulation of the essay. Critics tend to write as if the essay equates chastity with sexual abstinence, and sensuality with sexual activity. But this is not the case. Thoreau's formulation is that sexuality can be chaste or it can be sensual. According to his use of these terms, chastity is conduct that elevates; sensuality is conduct that degrades. Within Thoreau's sexual ethics, sexual abstinence is an option but not a requirement in pursuing a chaste life. But by his lights, abstinence per se does not ensure chastity. And marriage is certainly not something that takes over from chastity, as some of the contemporary discourses on chastity and abstinence seem to suggest. The Sex Respect program presents chastity within a model of heterosexual marriage in which abstinence is a pre-marital prescription and spousal sex is a marital prescription. This is contrary to Thoreau's view, for as he states, "Chastity is something positive, not negative," adding that it is "the virtue of the married especially" (Thoreau 1975, 274).

The same heteronormative assumptions may be the reason why critics have disregarded the essay's wordplay. Or perhaps they see the wordplay but dismiss it as Victorian euphemism, more evidence of symptomatic sexual anxiety. Whatever the reason, it is a significant oversight because punning and paradox are the means by which Thoreau chastises normative attitudes and behavior. Both punning and paradox are a kind of double-talk that serves the closet; both rhetorical devices allow a statement to be simultaneously inside and outside the closet. This inside/outside relation informs the particular epistemology of Thoreau's closet, which operates through a series of oppositions: open/secret; pure/impure; cold/warm; light/dark. The essay's privileging of what is open, pure, cold, and illuminated also informs Thoreau's transcendentalism, which universalizes the value of refusing to restrict meaning. The epistemology of his transcendental closet thus opens up and expands possibilities of truth, including sexual truths.

"Chastity and Sensuality": A Queer Exegesis

Puns abound in "Chastity and Sensuality," beginning with its opening line: "The subject of sex is a remarkable one." Remarkable, yes, but, as he explains, not *adequately* remarked on. Despite the fact that "its phenomena concern us so much, both directly and indirectly, and sooner or later, it occupies the thoughts of us all, yet all mankind, as it were, agree to be silent about it" (Thoreau 1975, 274). From a Foucauldian perspective, Thoreau's call for less silence about sexuality is counterpoised to the emerging deployment of sexuality, understood as a "political, economic, and technical incitement to talk about sex."[35] This deployment urges confessional discourse, an unbearing of the soul or psyche as the preeminent means for purging one's perverse desires. In terms of literature, we can see this deployment taking hold in Nathaniel Hawthorne's *The Scarlet Letter* with Arthur Dimmesdale's dramatic final act, a full confession before his congregation. In contrast, Thoreau challenges this mandate to confess, in both its religious and secular forms. For the silence about which Thoreau complains does not refer to a paucity of statements regarding sex, but to the lack of what he calls "genuine intercommunication," between even the "most intimate friends."

The invitation for Blake to "enlighten" him on whether his thoughts reveal a "peculiar defect" is thus a request for just such a dialogue between friends. This is, at least implicitly, a challenge to heterosexual privilege wherein the speaking of desire is reserved for opposite-sex relations. That privilege, in Thoreau's relationship with another friend, Ellery Channing, was compounded by Channing's habit of speaking of "sexual relations but jestingly."[36] For Thoreau such trivialization of sexuality is the antithesis of chastity. In other writings he expressed distaste for coarse jokes and outhouse graffiti. In other words, in urging more discussion of sexuality he urges neither religious confession nor disclosure of perversity—likely to elicit punishment—nor coarseness. The remarking of sex he calls for is, in effect, a re-making of sex.

Ironically, the silence he reproaches was borne out when "Chastity and Sensuality" was posthumously published. In the line that reads, "In a pure society, the subject of copulation would not be so often avoided—from shame and not from reverence, winked out of sight, and hinted at only," Emerson substituted the word *marriage* for *copulation* (Thoreau 1975, 274).[37] This bowdlerizing of Thoreau's words not only ruins the subsequent pun which follows in the assertion that "Men commonly couple with their idea of marriage a slight degree at least of sensuality" (274), it also interferes with Thoreau's scathing critique against conventional attitudes about sexuality and marriage. The charge he makes is not against sex, as some critics have said, but against the way that shame restricts sex: "If it cannot be spoken of for shame, how can it be acted of?" (Thoreau 1975, 274). Here he suggests that marriage itself is too often common, that is, beset with shame.

More poignant than ironic is the silence Thoreau opts for in this discussion. The following deletion occurs from his May 5, 1846, journal entry, from which the first part of the essay is drawn, almost verbatim: "I love men with the same distinction that I love woman—as if my friend were of some third sex—some other or stranger and still my friend."[38] As in the fable Aristophanes tells in the *Symposium*, the friend who is a "third sex" is a stranger but is not estranged. If they are both a "third sex," then, perhaps, each has found his long-lost "half." Instead of including this expression of desire for his third-sexed friend in "Chastity and Sensuality," Thoreau ruminates further on the status of avoidance. In place of shame-induced avoidance, he proposes that a reverential view of the subject of copulation might include it being "simply avoided, like the kindred mysteries."

This use of paradox to simultaneously denounce and praise avoidance characterizes the open/secret opposition. A chaste knowledge of sexuality makes it unnecessary to explain sexuality, since, like the "kindred mysteries," it is already in the open. In contrast, shame or sensual knowledge prompts ignorant and disdainful avoidance of the subject. "Common" heterosexuality is in the open, that is, accepted in public, and whispers or jokes or scribbles on the walls of the outhouse. These explicit references to shame here also suggest how Thoreau's earlier admission to Blake of his own shame might be better understood, again in light of asking for Blake's response to further his own education. As he states, "the education of man has hardly commenced." This is why they so often have nothing "worthy to say" about the subject of copulation (Thoreau 1975, 274).

Although there is no explicit complaint made in "Chastity and Sensuality" about heterosexual privilege and state-sanctioned marriage—and it would be most unlikely given its time—I read the essay as distinguishing between the legal institution of marriage, which legally sanctions opposite-sex couples only, and what Thoreau refers to as "true marriage." What he calls true marriage, true love, is neither the business of the state nor exclusive to opposite-sex couples. It is notable that his language never delimits "true marriage" to men and women. On one occasion when he explicitly refers to a woman as the recipient of love, he uses a plural pronoun, saying that "We must love our friend so much that she shall be associated with our purest and holiest thoughts alone" (Thoreau 1975, 276). This yields a rather odd effect; perhaps meant to evoke Blake within the general category of men, the inclusive use of the plural *we* and *our* with the singular *friend* produces a triangulation between the two men and the woman, evocative (for me at least) of the relationship between his brother John, himself, and Ellen Sewell.[39] Otherwise, the consistent use of plural pronouns *they*, *us*, and *we* is nongender-specific, and corresponds to his use of "the affectionate," or, in a punning vein, when he speaks of how "the parties incessantly stimulate each other to a loftier and purer life" (Thoreau 1975, 275). At one point, in referring to "when a youth embraces his betrothed virgin," he specifically uses a masculine pronoun but does not gender the recipient of his desire. At a crucial juncture, he provides a homoerotic analogy to indicate that a "man's social and spiritual discipline must answer to his corporeal. He must lean on a friend who has a hard breast, as he would lie on a hard bed" (275).

Oppositions between purity and impurity, coldness and warmth, and light and dark reinforce a sexual ethics in which chastity is an activity rather than a state of being. Although the practice of abstinence is raised, it applies only to beverages and not to sex; Thoreau states unequivocally that a man "must drink cold water for his only beverage" and applies this corporeal practice to a social and spiritual one, indicating that "he must not hear sweetened and colored words, but pure and refreshing truths" (Thoreau 1975, 275). The self-discipline that Thoreau insists is integral to chastity holds equally for the individual alone and as a member of "true marriage." Using metaphors of heat and cold, he opposes chastity to sloth. Valuable bodily warmth can be attained only by "healthful exercise" and spiritual warmth only from "noble deeds." But "cats and dogs and slothful persons" mistakenly think that sexuality's warmth is enough and hence they "hug the fire" (275). Since this warmth is at best sporadic—what he designates as lust—they need to seek the most constant warmth of "celestial love," which he aligns with the "cold affection of the sun reflected from fields of ice and snow, or his warmth in some wintry dell" (275). This reference to the sun with a masculine pronoun instead of an "it" gives a homoerotic hue to the comment even as it suggests the pleasure of deflected affection.

Thoreau's opposition between love and lust is a standard one in U.S. discourses on sexuality. But, unlike most of these dominant discourses, he does not associate lust with unmarried sexuality and love with married sexuality. And, contrary to what critics suggest, there is no indication that celestial love is to replace sexual activity. Nor is sexual activity a requirement of marriage.[40] The paradoxical insistence that love is cold parallels his assertion that one must "daily bathe in truth cold as spring water" (Thoreau 1975, 275). The constraints of closeted desire clarify the logic of this paradox, which runs like this: closeted love in some sense is always cold but no less true; spring water is true and pure; true love, therefore, must be pure and cold; closeted love may be the truest and purest love.

Using metaphors of bodily contamination, which were prevalent in the social reform movements of the day, and which, as Mary Douglas has suggested, mark a shift from the worship of God to a worship of nature, Thoreau comments on the "danger that we may stain and pollute one another" (276).[41] How can this be prevented? By "not accepting one another." Again, as the paragraph continues, readers find that the refusal he advocates is not a refusal of sexual embrace, but a refusal to accept one another's "lower natures." On this line of thought, the lower nature of humanity is a slothful, animal nature with no spiritual growth. Because "the affectionate" embrace each other "with an entire embrace," it is inevitable that they influence the character of one another. A common marriage would thus be akin to a kind of bestiality, a coupling of the human and the animal.

As with *Walden*'s condemnation of materialism, here he condemns the materialism of sexual relations as impure: "the *luxury* of affection—there's the danger." Thoreau's point is that marrying in order to legitimize sexual activity is a poor basis for marriage and a detriment to personal growth. He represents lust as a "brothel," a place which equates sex and money; accordingly, a marriage based on the "*luxury* of affection" turns the home into a brothel (Thoreau 1975, 276). One frequently cited instance of his view of marriage is when he kicked a skunk cabbage, saying to David Wasson, "There, marriage is like that."[42] Thoreau's judgment about the state of marriage might be harsh—but it is also an apt description of many marriages. Feminists throughout the nineteenth century used equally condemnatory language against marriage as a form of legal prostitution in their efforts to secure women's economic and social equality, the right to divorce and child custody. They too equated marriage with the "brothel," arguing that men's excessive animal instinct and brutishness forced women into degraded sexual relations.

As a model of chastity for humanity, Thoreau offers flowers. Critics have cited this as particularly symptomatic of Thoreau's sexual anxiety. Charles Anderson sees it as an "evasion of sex as a reality" and Robert Richardson claims that in this passage "Thoreau treats sex in outrageous botanical language."[43] If it were not delivered in a derogatory tone, I would agree with Richardson's use of "outrageous" to describe this passage. Despite some of its cloying sentiment, it is outrageous in its call for something clearly outside of heterosexist bounds of authority, namely an *open* expression of sexuality. Flowers, Thoreau says, offer our language "many pregnant symbols." Punning on the euphemisms of hymen penetration while reversing standard assumptions about it, he claims that "by an impure marriage the virgin is deflowered." A pure, true marriage, he implies, celebrates the flowering of bodies through an impregnation of spiritual life, which does not preclude sexual intercourse. To exemplify the "open and unsuspected beauty of all true marriage, when man's flowering season arrives," he quotes his own translation from J. Bilberg in "Amoenitates Botanicae," edited by Linnaeus. "The organs of generation which in the animal kingdom, are for the most part concealed by nature as if they were to be ashamed of, in the vegetable kingdom are exposed to the eyes of all; and, when the nuptials of plants are celebrated, it is wonderful what delight they afford to the beholder, refreshing the senses with the most agreeable color and the sweetest odor." (277) As Thoreau presents it, then, sensuous delight, chastity, and knowledge are antidotes to shame, sensuality, and ignorance.

F. O. Matthiessen's emphasis half a century ago on the importance of Thoreau's sensuousness, and its opposition to sensuality, bears repeating here. As he comments, "What separates Thoreau most from Emerson is his interest in the varied play of all his senses, not merely of the eye, a rare enough attribute in New England and important to dwell on since it is the crucial factor in accounting for the greater density of Thoreau's style."[44] In seeking the "*purely* sensuous," Matthiessen argues, Thoreau put a "checkrein" on his senses in order to aesthetically render his experience in words, which Matthiessen credits as the means by which he avoided "gliding away into a romantic reverie of escape."[45] This observation is closer in spirit to a closeting of desire than a sublimating of sexual energy. Thoreau's aesthetic principle corresponds, I believe, to his view that sensuous delight, though desirable, makes one susceptible to sensuality, which ultimately has the "odor of carrion" (Thoreau 1975, 277). Indeed, he goes on to ponder whether "evil spirits might corrupt the flowers, rob them of their fragrance and their fair hues, and turn their marriage into a secret shame and defilement?" True marriage, in other words, is threatened and degraded by common marriage.

Drawing on the double meaning of *intercourse*, sexual and verbal, Thoreau writes that "the intercourse of the sexes, I have dreamed, is incredibly beautiful, too fair to be remembered. I have had thoughts about it, but they are among the most fleeting and irrecoverable in my experience." This passage, reminiscent of Margaret Fuller's *Woman in the Nineteenth Century*, encapsulates the transcendental dialectic between the preexisting ideal and the earthly real, in which imagination brings the ideal and real together. Again paradox—in this case between (secret) memory and (openly expressed) imagination—allows out in the open what would otherwise be secret. Thoreau suggests that what is too fair to be remembered can still be imaginatively "re-membered." As he states in the accompanying essay on "Love": the "imagination never forgets; it is a re-membering" (Thoreau, 1975, 270).

The "intercourse of the sexes," which cannot be remembered except fleetingly, evokes the elided passage about the third sex, who is both stranger and friend, as well as Aristophanes' story of a divided self, a long search and reunion with one's same or opposite-sexed beloved. In explicit references to orgasm, Thoreau states that "in all perception of the truth there is a divine ecstasy, an inexpressible delirium of joy, as when a youth embraces his betrothed virgin. The ultimate delights of a true marriage are one with this." Truth and sex are thus kindred experiences. And both are a kind of "illumination." Thoreau's expressions of this view are admittedly idealized, that is, transcendentalized, but they are not antisexual. His descriptions are no more prudish or euphemistic than Hawthorne's in *The Scarlet Letter* or Melville's "Squeeze of the Hand." Since the line that follows the passage on the "delirium of joy" is about reproduction, it would seem logical that Thoreau is not, as Richard Lebeaux argues, actually justifying celibacy, although, as I have said, that is an option within this approach to chastity.[46] Referring back to the model of the flowers, he comments that the "womb is a most fertile soil." Significantly, and in direct contrast to heterosexist beliefs which see procreation as the only real justification for sexuality, Thoreau specifically designates reproduction as an "accompaniment" rather than an "end" to sexuality.

The final two paragraphs of "Chastity and Sensuality" set up an opposition between two approaches to human "improvement." One is eugenically informed biological reproduction, which Thoreau dismisses as mere replication, and the other is spiritual reproduction, which he deems as actual "improvement."[47] Rejecting the views of the eugenic-minded social reformers of his time, he remarks that "Some have asked if the stock of men could not be improved,—if they could not be bred as cattle" (Thoreau 1975, 277). For Thoreau, this ostensible improvement breeds just the opposite result, for eugenically improving the "stock of men" is maintaining humanity at the level of animal stocks. The Neo-Malthusian goal was akin to slavery's treatment and breeding of human beings as if livestock. By contrast, he proposes that the biological reproduction of children should follow the way of "aspirations." He concludes with the following passage: "Nature abhors repetition. Beasts merely propagate their kind; but the offspring of noble men and women will be superior to themselves, as their aspirations are. By their fruits ye shall know them." He thus transvalues biblical discourse to invoke the transcendentalist principles of individual growth and the fruits of fertile imagination. In doing so, he redresses a key tenet of the system of normative heterosexuality, for, on his view, biological reproduction is valuable only if it follows the path of individual aspiration.

Establishing a Genealogy of Sexual Morality

From a Thoreauvian perspective, millennialist concepts of sexuality and chastity have too little respect for pleasures, bodies, and desires. Indeed, *Sex Respect* is a misnomer. As a program of education, it shuts down knowledge. As a discussion of chastity, it promotes the negation of desire rather than its "loftier delights." As a homogenizing system of morality, it undermines the variegation of sexuality. The value of looking to Thoreau's contrasting stance toward sexuality is not to promote it as a singular form of chastity, but rather to see it as one branch of an elaborate genealogy of sexual morality within the United States.[48] There is far more work to be done in tracing the various, often conflicting, discourses on chastity, and more ways of envisioning chastity. Such investigations need to be vigilant in questioning the normative assumptions— often a form of heterosexual electism—that we, as investigators, bring to our objects of study. A skeptical approach to compulsory heterosexuality reveals the ways in which our systems of classification objectify and endorse what we look at. In this regard, what is worth emulating is Thoreau's declared aspiration, with which I began this essay: "I desire that there may be as many different persons in the world as possible."[49] In our own research and thinking about sexual morality, and especially in teaching about sexuality in schools, we would do well to follow that path, seeking a skeptical way to enable different desires to speak their names.

*Corruption. The surest way to corrupt a youth
is to instruct him to hold in higher esteem those
who think alike than those who think differently.*
—Nietzsche, Axiom 297, The Dawn

5 COERCIVE PURITY: THE DANGEROUS PROMISE OF APOCALYPTIC MASCULINITY

In the final decade of the final century of the second millennium of the Christian era, a new form of apocalyptic masculinity emerged. Combining Christian fundamentalism, New Age fervor, and sports rally fever, the evangelical Christian men's movement called Promise Keepers used their slogan, "A man's man is a godly man," to advance a dual agenda: to help men regain leadership of their families and to help them forge Christian nationhood in the New Era.

As an organization, Promise Keepers exhibited exceptional skill for marshalling millennialist potency. Officially beginning in 1991, within just a few years, they were able to gather upwards of fifty thousand fellow worshipers at a time for rallies lasting up to fourteen hours over the course of two days. In their peak year, 1996, more than twenty different cities around the country hosted such rallies, bringing together an estimated 1 million men and producing a robust annual budget of $120 million.[1] In 1997, at least half a million men made a pilgrimage to the nation's capital to "Stand in the Gap" for the Lord. By 1998, however, this new brand of evangelicalism—a postmodern Great Awakening with a "men only" sign on the door—had met serious financial difficulty.[2] Once rally attendance started to fall in 1997, the organization decided to stop charging admission to their rallies. The official word was that this was an effort to "Open the gates in '98" by removing financial barriers, but it was also expedient if the momentum of the rallies was to be regained. The result was a financial shortfall, forcing a temporary layoff of its entire staff and turning to volunteers to meet their schedule of nineteen more rallies for the rest of the year. Since the admission fees brought in over 70 percent of the organization's income, the shift was significant. By Easter 1998, donations had offset the crisis, allowing Promise Keepers to continue its work by organizing men-only rallies in every state capitol to greet the first day of the new millennium.[3]

Whatever their third-millennium status proves to be, Promise Keepers may be understood as both a cause and effect of millennialism on American culture. What should skeptics make of this configuration of apocalypse? This chapter addresses that question by analyzing Promise Keepers as a case study in apocalyptic cultural practice. Exploring the history and techniques of the Promise Keepers reveals a great deal about the workings of apocalypticism and millennialism in the contemporary United States. At the outset, I want to indicate that my research left me, at best, ambivalent about Promise Keepers. On the one hand, it is undeniable that a large number of men today experience personal pain, frustration, and discontent about what it means to live *as a man*. As a feminist and a mother of two adult sons, I am in sympathy with this view, especially since Promise Keepers accentuates men's self-transformation. On the other hand, it is equally indisputable that Promise Keepers promotes social inequality by insisting on hierarchical gender roles and compulsory heterosexuality. They could emphasize self-transformation in the name of gender and sexual equality, but they have chosen not to. They have chosen instead to lead men down a path of enmity, in the name of millennialist love. Furthermore, their goal of forging a Christian nation is one more crack in the wall of separation of church and state.[4] My overall assessment is that the promises made by Promise Keepers threaten democratic freedom.

Given this assessment, the remarkable rise of Promise Keepers warrants some skeptical revelations about the organization and what it espouses. Its rapid national sweep prompted me to pose certain questions in the process of my inquiry. Psychological questions readily sprang to mind: What perceived needs were being tapped and/or met through this new men's movement? Structural questions followed: What organizational and economic arrangements enabled the Promise Keepers to grow exponentially in so few years? And, crucially, what social-political consequences have ensued, and might ensue, from their efforts? But to my mind the most important question—and the one that helps illuminate the others—is: Why, during the 1990s did a *fundamentalist religious* organization fire the imagination of so many men from across this nation?[5] At least part of that answer and the moving force of this book is that this historical moment is particularly susceptible to millennialist belief.

Given the time we live in, this is not surprising. With the approach of the millennium the sense of an impending end to the world as we know it fuels the millennialist expectation that with the end will come a new era of perfection. Those feelings however, won't necessarily erode when numbers replace the zeroes. Millennialist manhood is, therefore, cause for concern well into the third millennium. Marked as it is by twin features of redemption and demonization, apocalyptic logic will continue to polarize camps between a victimized elect and an odious enemy. Within this dynamic, the logic of apocalypse can be analyzed through three primary modes: the divine, a metaphysical belief system that ranges from fundamentalist religion to New Age thought; the technological, which sees technology as bringing either catastrophe or salvation to humanity; and the ironic, which operates through postmodern apathy or cynical self-interest.[6] As a discourse, contemporary apocalypse is often a mix of these modes, which makes it internally contradictory yet insistently absolutistic.

Promise Keepers combines the first two of these modes with a slight tint of the third. Briefly put, its blend of premillennialist and New Age thought functions squarely within the divine mode. Its internet dissemination of information across the globe and video savvy draw on the technological mode. In regard to the ironic mode, while Promise Keepers tend to be more earnest and sincere than most ironic apocalypticians, an emphasis on personal transformation steers members away from involvement with certain forms of political activism and links the organization to a generalized apathy over issues of poverty and racism. At the same time, Promise Keepers exhibits a kind of duplicity characteristic of ironic apocalypse's cynical self-interest: Certain political affiliations have been concealed and denied through an insistence that "Promise Keepers does not have a political agenda."[7]

In regard to understanding the group's political effects, I want to clarify the ways in which Promise Keepers fuels anti-feminist and homophobic attitudes and behavior. This is particularly egregious because Promise Keepers has incorporated the criticism of absent fathers and emotionally diminished manhood developed by feminism and the gay movement, yet it has turned these appropriations into denunciations of each. Ultimately what I want to show is how Promise Keepers, in the name of leading men to manly Christianity, produces what I call "coercive purity." The Promise Keepers' pursuit of purity of body and soul creates a faultline in members' masculine identity that divides between scapegoating nonpure others and fearing that impurity within themselves. This dynamic may be likened to the way the concept of purity was deployed by eugenic-minded scientists and legislators in the early part of this century to denounce Eastern European immigrants as genetically impure. Current efforts to stave off immigration focus on the purity of the English language. In the Promise Keepers' formulation, operating through a Christian model of internal temptation, purity is used to demonize homosexuals and feminists; although much of the emphasis is on self-coercion, the concept also functions to coerce others toward a fundamentalist-mandated concept of purity. In each instance, those deemed impure are scapegoated as a threat to the pure community. Whether this scapegoating erupts in violence, which is a potential threat within apocalyptic groups, or fuels legislative oppression, which has already occurred and is on their agenda, the foundational beliefs of the Promise Keepers breed injustice.

In order to grasp more fully the ways that Promise Keepers beliefs forge links between social injustice, self-loathing, and coercive purity, at the end of this chapter I return briefly to Tony Kushner's take on apocalyptic masculinity in *Angels in America: A Gay Fantasia on National Themes*. Kushner's play appeared in the same years of the Promise Keepers' founding and growth. It too has reached large audiences through its Broadway production and national tour. Like the Promise Keepers' rallies, *Angels in America* provides a spectacle prompting reflection on the pain of men's lives, set within a backdrop of apocalyptic urgency. But unlike Promise Keepers, *Angels* submits not only the mandates of traditional masculinity but also apocalypticism itself to skeptical examination.

The Life and Times of the Apocalyptic Male Subject

A skeptical genealogy of the apocalyptic male subject helps to illuminate the power/knowledge relations of apocalypticism. As I indicated earlier, this approach challenges the assumptions that apocalyptic history holds most dear, namely, that history unfolds from a single origin, links together through an unambiguous chain of cause and effect, and culminates in an end-time that has been foreordained.[8] In contrast to that view, skeptical genealogy examines history through its vicissitudes, as a mix of unexpected beginnings, multiple causes, and myriad effects. This is not to say that there is no order or continuity to be found, since entrenched power formations certainly impose orders of gender, sexuality, race, and class on culture. It is, rather, a way of dismantling those normative categories of order and hierarchy. Genealogy is thus a politically committed perspective.[9] Most crucially, it helps establish the ways in which apocalyptic discourses and practices have promulgated male supremacy, homophobia, and a vilification of certain racial and ethnic differences.

The double-edged point I want to stress is that the dominant narrative of order in this country has been, since colonization, an apocalyptic one and that apocalypticism has been one, if not *the*, predominant mode of antidemocratic belief and behavior. Phillip Greven's work is especially significant in this regard because he has shown correlations between apocalyptic belief systems and corporal punishment, indicating a spiral of biblically sanctioned abuse that gives rise to an adult willingness to inflict pain on children in the name of discipline and see punishment as a proper means of upholding order and obedience within families and for society in general.[10] This is relevant to the Promise Keepers in a number of ways. Even though a great deal of Promise Keepers rhetoric emphasizes love over wrath, it maintains the fundamentalist orientation toward the justified punishment of hell. The men who gather at the rallies are of the generations that Greven shows to be very likely to have received physical punishment from their parents. As he indicates, fundamentalist ministers from Billy Graham to James Dobson have argued for corporal punishment as a necessary means to stave off the eternal punishment of hell. Greven demonstrates persuasively that such beliefs give rise to adult psyches that suffer the scars of this abuse. Others—Paul Boyer, Charles Strozier, and Robert Jay Lifton, in particular—have clarified just how significant religious fundamentalism has been to this nation's history and its costs to the psychological well-being of those who live within the fixed self-framework of apocalypticism.

I am arguing, further, that apocalypse constitutes a regime of truth that blurs religious and secular lines, informing a range of beliefs and practices that include popular culture, fashion, science, social science, technology, and so on. Consider this popular culture example of apocalypse, which, though innocuous enough, from a genealogical perspective shows the intricate connections between disciplinary power, truth, and—in this case, male—subjectivity: Marvel comics' "Archangel II, an action toy figure based on a comic book character."[11] Here is what the back of the box has to say about him: "As the high-flying Angel, Warren Worthington III was one of the original members of the X-Men. Years later, Worthington's real wings were dissected, replaced with razor-sharp wings of steel, and he was transformed into Archangel, one of the four Horsemen of the Apocalypse. Now, having fought against the conditioning that tainted and turned him into a living weapon, Archangel has embraced his humanity and strives to regain the purity that once surrounded him."[12]

With just a touch of qualification over the literal or metaphorical status of Worthington's wings, this could be a description of a Promise Keeper. It is a description that should be read in light of what is referred to these days as the "crisis in masculinity": a confusion and precariousness in men's gender identity, which corresponds to the postmodern acceleration of many cultural uncertainties, including declining economic power under late capitalism and a drop in the United States' status as supreme imperialist power. Both the crisis in and the attempt to "rehabilitate" masculinity seem to be occurring most intensely for the generation of men who grew up in the X-Men era, men who probably read these top-selling comics of the past few decades and who, as fathers, are likely to have children who play with these figures and watch them on television.[13] These men, like their comic counterparts, have been deeply affected not only by growing economic and military insecurity but also by feminism and other civil rights movements of the past four decades.[14] The promises of restored order in apocalypse offer a ready-made way not only to assuage their anxiety and uncertainty but also to rectify perceived losses.[15]

Along with practices of punishment and schooling, genealogical investigation includes cultural artifacts like the X-Men and practices such as play to help understand how we become subjects—that is, how we incorporate or literally *embody* power relations and belief systems that then emerge as our sense of self. Subjectivity derives from certain repetitions of gesture, dress, posture, and movement, often performed according to regular time schedules, that discipline our bodies and minds. Genealogy, in other words, offers a historical dimension to psychological models of selfhood that otherwise lack adequate understanding about the relationship between power formations and selfhood.[16] When a child plays with Archangel II, he—and for a host of reasons, it is most likely a he—is in training as a masculine subject. Grasping the figure in his hand, it becomes an extension of his own body learning how to whip it about through aggressive and militaristic gestures, throw it against the enemy, and raise his voice in shouts of authority and threat. The incoherences and contradictions within contemporary masculinity are also on display in Archangel and hence transmitted as well. His Terminator-like muscularity reinforces the notion of the masculine body as a weapon even as he strives to overcome his former self. It is probably a sign of postmodern cynicism for Marvel to employ the language of social psychology and feminism in Archangel's utopian renunciation of violent conditioning, but it is nonetheless featured and thus imparted. The doubled desire to take on and escape masculinity is encapsulated by the instruction on the box which indicates that you can "squeeze legs together to activate wing-flapping action."

Such a toy is both symptomatic and productive of current confusions about masculinity. Attempts to quell these confusions can take many forms, ranging from feminist transformation to aggressive masculinist backlash. Given the conditions of today's society, the latter is a significant threat. As Robert Jay Lifton and Charles Strozier have documented, the violent imagery and fixed self-framework of apocalypticism damages the psychological well-being of those who live within its grip.[17] To put it even more bluntly, the Book of Revelation and the secular forms that incorporate its imagery provide both a paradigm of masculinist fantasy and a contemporary training manual in apocalyptic justification of violence. Recurrently, this psychological disposition has been systematically aimed against women and a variety of cultural others, including homosexuals, blacks, Arabs and Jews.

I am not exonerating these "others"—they too can be and have been apocalyptic. But I am stating the feminist point so starkly because it is too often ignored.[18] As I argue more fully in the next chapter, the gender and sexual dynamic of the Book of Revelation celebrates violence between men and against women.[19] We see this celebration through the 144,000 men who "follow the Lamb" and who *because* they are "not defiled with women," are ushered into the New Jerusalem (Revelation 14:3–4). We see violence against women enacted in the punishment of Jezebel, who has dared to be a teacher and has challenged men's sexual prerogative: "Behold I will cast her into a bed, and them that commit adultery with her into great tribulation, except they repent of their deeds. And I will kill her children with death" (Revelation 2:22–23). We see it with the Whore of Babylon, the feminized trope through which evil and corruption are depicted. Her punishment is to be made "desolate and naked," to have her flesh eaten and then burned (Revelation 17:16). And we see continuities of such violence throughout history in the systematic rape and slaughter of women and their children as part of apocalyptically inspired warfare.

Such reminders may well sound hyperbolic given Promise Keepers' saccharine-sounding rhetoric. But it is important to see the spectrum of apocalyptic masculinity which, whether moderate or extreme, defines itself as pure by designating and demonizing categories of impurity. As Robert Jay Lifton argues in regard to ideological totalism, "by defining and manipulating the criteria of purity, and then by conducting an all-out war upon impurity, the ideological totalists create a narrow world of guilt and shame."[20] A genealogy of the apocalyptic male subject makes visible these otherwise hidden branches of connection between biblical Truth, demonization of women's sexuality and homosexuality, and obsession with punishment exacted in this world or in hell. The Promise Keepers' brand of masculinity, through its insistence on purity, sets men up to pursue an impossible eradication of desire, fueling that desire through evocation of its treachery while condemning its expression.

The Political Fields of a Capitalist Lord

During their peak years of revenue, Promise Keepers built a large staff in a few short years at their Denver headquarters (up to 345 at one point). More than 20,000 men also worked in a local capacity within the organization's network of state offices. Organizationally, the top staff included a president, Randy Phillips, whose tax returns placed him at over $132,000 per year, and several department heads whose salaries were reported to be in the $75,000 to $100,000 range.[21] Until the 1998 decision to stop charging for admission, the most significant sums of money came from the rallies. The price of admission was around $60. Millions more were raised through the selling of Promise Keepers kitsch such as coffee mugs and t-shirts as well as publications. Although Promise Keepers is a men's movement, from the outset women did a substantial amount of work in the organization—as unpaid volunteers.[22]

In their heyday, the Promise Keepers' sizeable budget facilitated an effective public relations effort, which in turn, of course, raised money. News coverage over the first six years, whether in religious or secular newspapers, had a canned quality dependent on materials circulated by the group. Official publications indicate strict oversight by the central organization. The first Promise Keepers book, titled *Seven Promises of a Promise Keeper*, is a compilation of essays and speeches by leaders in the organization. The second, *The Power of a Promise Kept*, is a series of thirteen "life stories" as told by Gregg Lewis, dealing variously with issues of self-doubt, failing marriages, and addiction to pornography. Ultimately these are stories of defeating the demons, restoring love, and attaining purity. *Go the Distance*, the third book, continues in a similar vein, lauding the spiritual intimacy and male bonding fostered in rallies and small group meetings.

From the time of the Promise Keepers' founding, controversy centered over whether the organization sported a political agenda. Official word insists on the group's political neutrality. In terms of their overt effort toward ideological transformation, this is obviously inaccurate. The claim, of course, ignores that definition of *political* to focus on the more narrow definition of legislative politics and electoral involvement. But this is not borne out either, considering their organizational affiliations enabled them to farm out their political agenda to other groups. The most important connection in this respect is with psychologist Dr. James C. Dobson and his Colorado-based organization known as Focus on the Family, founded in 1977 and now with an annual budget of $90 million. Dobson is one of the contributors to the first Promise Keepers book and his organization published the subsequent books. Through his nationally syndicated daily radio program and several magazines, Dobson provides a forum for virulent antiabortion leaders like Randall Terry and antigay activists like Gene Antonio, author of *The AIDS Cover-Up*. Dobson's group has consistently provided resources for affiliates that work actively in legislative efforts to promote Religious Right sex education for public schools and to repeal gay and lesbian civil rights protection.[23] Additional links suggest that Promise Keepers have a clear right-wing political agenda: several board members also belong to the Council for National Policy. Beyond that Promise Keepers sponsored Jerry Falwell for speaking events.[24] In short, a look at the leaders of the men who would be leaders provides ample evidence of overt political work and it is, at best, disingenuous, to say otherwise.

Regardless of the financial status of the central organization, Promise Keepers' well-orchestrated grassroots effort has laid the groundwork for ongoing dissemination of its political perspective. The rallies facilitated the establishment of local ministries by recruiting team leaders who have in turn organized small groups charged with counseling each other and learning how to spread the word by forming more groups. This kind of Tupperware-style, home-sales entrepreneurial model has been used effectively in concert with televangelism for years, and Promise Keepers capitalized on it. Promise Keepers' use of Internet technology has also activated the globalization of fundamentalist belief: weekly cyberspace meetings for men of Promise Keeper persuasion have been established on several continents.

Looking for Mr. Apocalypse

By far the most distinguishing feature of Promise Keepers was their innovative twist on evangelical revivalism. In this respect they bear comparison to earlier revival movements in the United States. In fact, they billed themselves as part of this lineage by referring to their endeavor as the next Great Awakening or the Grand Awakening.[25] Yet both their ambitions and their successes far exceeded the capacity of the old-time revival tent. Much like the urban evangelical gatherings of the late nineteenth century organized by Dwight L. Moody and elevated to an artform of televangelism by Billy Graham in our times, Promise Keepers gatherings took place in large football stadiums equipped with giant video screens.[26]

Over the years, Promise Keepers rallies remained pretty similar. Here is a sketch from a *Los Angeles Times* reporter who attended one of the early gatherings, in 1994:

> Lights flood the infield at Anaheim Stadium. It is opening night.
>
> From the left-field bleachers a shout, reminiscent of a high school cheer, goes out: "I love Jesus, yes I do! I love Jesus, how 'bout you?" The mood is celebratory and, in the spirit of men, vaguely competitive. From across the stadium comes the right field's still louder rejoinder: "We love Jesus, yes we do! We love Jesus, how 'bout you?"
>
> Soon, the 50,000 men rise to their feet as the band strikes up a rousing, rocking rhythm, "Let the Walls Fall Down!"
>
> One hundred thousand uplifted hands in perfect synchronization sway like palm fronds in the wind. Like a well-tuned engine they compress the air, exploding in rhythmic concussions of clapping that sound like a locomotive barreling down the tracks.
>
> These older men with paunches, middle-aged men with graying temples, young men with complexions as fair as the dawn are entering Robert Bly's woods. They are singing songs around the campfire. They are beating drums, summoning the wild man from within. But this time, Jesus is their guide.
>
> The citadel of male stoicism and self-reliance begins to crack. Men put their arms around each other like boyhood pals. Brotherhood is replacing competition.[27]

I cite this description for a couple of reasons. For one thing, its tone shifts into sympathy as the men become emotionally responsive. I think it is important to keep this in mind as a value of Promise Keepers even as I am critical of the group for the way their male bonding constructs enemies. Secondly, this report of the emergence of Promise Keepers out of the waning "Iron John" movement and its narration of the basic formula of the rallies was replicated by most media coverage. Both the writings of Promise Keepers themselves and of the news media— whether religious or secular, print or visual—indicated that a typical rally opened with call and response, moved to clapping and singing, and then to speakers who urged men to confront their deep emotional wounds and to grasp how their personal suffering has led them to be absent or uncaring fathers, sons, and brothers.

In the first several years, some of the messages were expressly political, as with the 1994 speech of the Reverend E. V. Hill who called the American Civil Liberties Union (ACLU) satanic, declared abortion an epidemic, and decried the teaching of evolution.[28] Such overt political rhetoric was eventually toned down after criticism from other denominations. Many chants had a decidedly aggressive face. Shouts of "Hit him! Hit him! Hit him!" accompanied by fist-clenching no doubt raise collective energies to a militant pitch, and were deemed acceptable because the *him* in question was the devil.[29] When the D.C. million man Stand in the Gap gathering occurred, however, this aggressive outlet had also been watered down, probably for televised viewing; the result, I believe, was a weakening of Promise Keeper appeal. Most of the rallies culminated with an appearance by Bill McCartney, a former head coach of the University of Colorado football team and the man credited with founding Promise Keepers. Typically, McCartney would return to the call-and-response device that opened the rally to emphasize the triumph of the believer: "There's nothing I want more in life than to serve Jesus Christ, because I want Almighty God's favor on me. How about you?"[30]

McCartney, a former Roman Catholic who became a member of Denver's charismatic Vineyard Church, exemplifies the paradoxes of millennialism as expressed in fundamentalist Christian brotherhood. He calls for men to be more loving and caring, yet his rhetoric turns on warrior metaphors and an evocation of violence, as when he proclaims,

"We have been *in* a war but not *at* war! If we are to make a difference, it will require much more than we've been doing until now."[31] He beseeches men to become more loving toward each other but in a 1992 news conference condemned "homosexuality [as] an abomination against Almighty God."[32] He urges men to reclaim their manhood but espouses surrender as part of God's divine plan: "It could be that God has brought us to Boulder to oversee our death. Become dead and open yourself up to him."[33]

McCartney's often-repeated use of his own life story to represent the theme of becoming dead to one's un-Christian values is selectively candid and slightly self-aggrandizing in the spirit of Nietzsche's insight about the contradictory pride of self-renunciation. His confessions about failing to be a leader in his own home and his faltering marriage were standard fare at the rallies. So too his disclosures about his unmarried teenage daughter becoming pregnant by one of his football players. That story took an especially dramatic turn in the telling because the father of this grandchild died from stomach cancer, but not before McCartney had aided his conversion to Christ.[34] The story as told thus activates a struggle for male purity in which a woman's body becomes the battlefield, the territory for the victor to claim. Actually, Kristy McCartney had two children by two different members of her father's football team, one in 1988 when she was nineteen years old by Sal Aunese, who died, and another in 1993 by Shannon Clavelle when she was twenty-four.[35] Of course, this version lacks the emotional drama of the conversion narrative. McCartney's story also took something of a contradictory turn regarding his resignation of a highly successful coaching position (at a salary of $350,000 per year). Most Promise Keepers would not be in a financial position to follow suit; hence he distinguished himself as Promise Keeper *par excellence*, capitalizing on his action by saying he did so in order to devote more time to his family while also expanding Promise Keepers.[36] His wife's disclosures in 1997 about the shakiness of their marriage confirmed marital problems but cast a less favorable light on McCartney's trajectory toward family dedication.[37]

As the driving force behind Promise Keepers, Bill McCartney's values were also disseminated in *New Man* magazine. Like McCartney's rhetoric and the rallies' rituals, the magazine's messages oscillate between love and hatred—in the name of purity. An article entitled "The Silent Struggle" in the September/October 1995 issue is a case in point. It tells the story of several Christian men struggling against homosexuality. As with many of the articles throughout, readers are assured of the manliness of the men in question. In this case, we are introduced first to John, who at 240 pounds is "built like a starting linebacker." Although we are not given the outcome of John's struggle, several others are cited who are triumphant in their defeat of this biblical sin. The testimony of Jeff Konrad, a former homosexual who had lived with another man for eleven years but who is "now married with two children," reveals a link between rigid gender roles, the proclaimed sinfulness of homosexuality, and the theater of self-loathing: "I used to hate myself. I felt ugly and feminine. Today I can look in the mirror and like what I see. God has made me into a man." The rest of the article encourages prayer as a means of struggle, male mentoring as an acceptable way to gain "same-sex intimacy" and provides a list of organizations and books that can help provide "freedom from homosexuality."[38]

Just as Promise Keepers associate heterosexuality with purity and homosexuality with impurity, so too does this binary reinforce strict gender roles. In the first Promise Keepers book, Tony Evans, a pastor and also the chaplain of the Dallas Mavericks basketball team, argues that the national crisis in families has occurred because of "the feminization of the American male," by which he means "a misunderstanding of manhood that has produced a nation of 'sissified' men who abdicate their role as spiritually pure leaders, thus forcing women to fill the vacuum."[39] Clearly, from Evans's perspective, when women have filled this vacuum, they have gone seriously awry—in ways that look a lot like feminism. For Promise Keepers, feminist insistence on equality in the family challenges the divinely-mandated plan of male leadership and female submission.

At least as worrisome as this enforced gender hierarchy is Promise Keepers' disregard of the issue of domestic violence. Given Phillip Greven's work on the widespread use of corporeal punishment within Christian fundamentalism, this absence constitutes a failure to come to grips with a dire problem. There was no mention in the three books or the group's study series guide of this sizeable problem within U.S. family life, despite the fact that the life stories in the second book include such chapters as "A Promise Keeper Strengthens His Marriage" and "A Promise Keeper Loves and Disciplines His Children." This lack of focus on domestic abuse serves to exacerbate the urgent concern that feminists have repeatedly raised in correlating male violence in the home with the combined factors of assumed male supremacy and declining male cultural status. Instead, readers are offered a questionable transformation through the life story of Warren Risniak, touted as a father who learns about loving and disciplining his children. The "real changes" that are recited include the fact that the "entire family sits down together for breakfast and supper almost every day" and that his children "feel involved with their dad." The nexus of their involvement? "They all get a kick out of stuffing envelopes and helping send out his business mailings. To recognize their help, Warren got all of them their own business cards."[40]

A dubious race understanding accompanied the Promise Keepers' clouded vision of family life. Women-led homes within the African American community are blamed for undermining national (read male) security. Or, as Tony Evans, himself an African American, puts it, "in the black community, . . . women run the show to an alarming degree."[41] Again, for Promise Keepers the danger lies in the way that women feminize men, a stance that leads away from recognizing that poverty for African American women, and women in general, does indeed threaten the well-being of the nation as a whole. As June Jordan has indicated, "the welfare of the majority [women] will determine the welfare of the state."[42] There is a particular irony in the racial stance of Promise Keepers' literature, since they explicitly called for "racial reconciliation," appointed minority men to the board, and highlighted African American speakers, like Evans, and singers at the rallies. Despite such efforts, and the multicultural impression of their publicity videos, minority attendance remained around 7 percent (with the exception of the New York City-based rallies where it was much higher).[43] This inconsistency between goal and results may serve as a sign of how seriously Promise Keepers failed to grasp minority issues, especially the social and economic sources of the feminization of poverty. In this light, their appropriation of the name PUSH (Jesse Jackson's organization, "People United to Serve Humanity) as their acronym for "Pray Until Something

Happens" comes off as more of a ploy of co-optation than an effort for reconciliation; the shift from service to prayer is a telling reminder that, in regard to social justice, Promise Keepers cast their eyes on the deferred prize.

Such an appropriation is even clearer in regard to the language of gender. The chapter in which the acronym PUSH appears concludes with a striking usurpation of female reproduction: "Promise Keepers have become impregnated with personal revival. Our changed lives are obvious. Like a woman who is pregnant and nearing the end of her term, we Christian men are about to burst forth with the coming of the Lord in ways we have never experienced."[44] Lest the men confuse such a bursting forth with being (God forbid) feminine, "real men" masculinity is reinforced by organizing members into follow-up groups for purposes of training them in "progressive sanctification."[45] Their grassroots organizational method is spelled out in *Seven Promises of a Promise Keeper*. Readers are urged "to work through the book for at least eight weeks in a small group of men—three to five is an ideal number."[46] At the end of each of the chapters written by "proven warriors," specific instructions are provided. As a cross between a social science questionnaire and a catechism, these begin with a personal evaluation in which a man ranks himself on a scale of 1 to 10, "with 1 being very weak and 10 being perfect." That is followed by an explicit instruction to pray together about the issue at hand, questions that the men in each group should discuss as well, and a biblical verse to memorize. Finally there is an assigned activity—writing a prayer, for example—to be practiced during the week until the next group meeting. Promise Keepers' kits provide even more extensive guidance for work in small groups, with instructions for forty-five one-hour sessions geared to four to ten men in attendance.

Such small group meetings have been the tried and true of many other mass movement efforts, from Marxist cells to feminist consciousness-raising groups. Combined with large rallies, they can be quite effective as a means of spreading whatever teachings a group wishes to promote. This disciplinary technique, which combines confessional elements with exercises for self-transformation, has its roots and its greatest successes in the dissemination of the apocalyptic vision within Christianity. This is in part because of the promise of perfectibility and the drama of seeing one's group as persecuted. It is hardly surprising, at the turn of the millennium and as media-fed contemporary life continues to have a dizzying effect, that these groups create a sense of stability and bonding. It is even less surprising, given the dulling effect of late-capitalist work life, that Promise Keepers rallies' generation of emotion and cathartic outlet proved so compelling.

What is troubling—whether Marxist, feminist, or fundamentalist—is the feverish dogmatism of the apocalyptic approach. The thread between purity and self-righteousness stretches thin and snaps easily. When applied programmatically to teachings against "the feminization of the American male," to strategies for taking back leadership of the family, or to ways to eradicate abortion and homosexuality, coercive purity contaminates the democratic principle and practice of equality.

"God . . . (Thunderclap)/ He Isn't Coming Back"

What if, at the inception of the third millennium, the transformation of men were to take a different turn? What if men began to take both seriously and skeptically, that is, non-dogmatically, the challenge from *Angels in America* that they become tellers of truth in a new way, recognizing their own buried fears and betrayals as well as their personal and public complicities? Like a Promise Keepers rally, *Angels* beckons to men to embrace one another in love. But, contrary to a Promise Keepers event, *Angels* shows the destructiveness to self of the kind of love that comes from sources of hatred or disdain, the kind that blithely claims to "love the sinner, hate the sin," the kind that blinds itself to exclusions inherent in forging a Christian nation.[47]

Of all of the characters in *Angels*, the one that most reminds me of a Promise Keeper is Louis Ironson, ironically, since, unlike Joe Pitt who espouses Promise Keeper values, Louis, is probably the least likely to join up. Though I have seen evangelical Christian ads on New York subways which insists that Jews can become more Jewish by converting to Christian fundamentalism, I don't think Louis would be convinced. His blend of cynicism, atheism, and Jewish cultural affiliation puts him at some remove from evangelical belief. But, as I noted in the Chapter 2 on teaching apocalypse, Louis Ironson is a man who both desires to understand himself and his motives better and also to evade that knowledge. Guilt, especially the public disclosure of it, facilitates that emotional and ethical standstill. Although he struggles to be responsible to others, and is in torment over abandoning his lover, Prior, his own sense of being abandoned overrides his sense of obligation. This swirls into more guilt and agony over his inability to sustain a loving relationship. Initially at least, when he becomes sexually intimate with Joe Pitt, he feels that he has overcome these shortcomings. He empathizes with Joe's own struggle of conscience from having left his wife Harper when she too is in need. Although Promise Keeper teachings emphasize loyalty to one's wife, the examples from the publications and rally sermons are rarely a strong test of being a caring husband over a long period of time for a partner who is suffering deeply. Instead, a focus on male empathy, made visible and palpable through tears and embraces, shifts rapidly into self-congratulation about the transformation that has occurred, not through ongoing ethical activity but rather the conviction that one has seen the empathetic light.

A work of skeptical imagination such as *Angels* can be helpful for prying open the canned sentiments of Promise Keepers morality Lite, replacing slogans and vague declarations of love and leadership with moral activities that minister to others' physical, emotional, and spiritual well-being. An imagination fueled with apocalyptic righteousness burns away the possibility of reconceiving morality for a world in which it often feels like "he"—whether that he is God, or one's father or lover or friend—isn't coming back. Belief systems like Promise Keepers thrive on the emotions of wounded sons who feel abandoned, offering them an immediacy of solace at the rallies. To reinforce this fleeting taste of reconciliation, it promises the far greater enveloping embrace of God the Father. The cost of this reunion, however, is acceptance of a narrow fundamentalist moral universe proclaiming an absolute Truth for all.

The other day I imagined a Promise Keepers rally in which a performance of *Angels in America* comprised the two-day event. Begun facetiously, my reverie took a serious and then somber turn. I found myself wondering just what it would take for these self-proclaimed godly men to ask themselves new ethical questions. In place of apocalyptic oratory, music, chants, and prayer, I tried to envision a stadium full of men bearing witness to the meaningfulness of Prior Walter's blessing—men who suddenly realized what it means to have granted *less* life to gay men and lesbians; men who had undergone a transformation more vital and loving than anything envisioned by Bill McCartney. As new men, might not they grasp, perhaps for the first time in their own lives, what it means to create more life?

To be truthful, on that day my imagination could not take me as far as I wanted it to, which was to see this transformation carried forth as an ongoing and everyday challenge to apocalyptic fundamentalism. I just could not get my mind around the vision of Promise Keepers promising to embrace women's equality, support minority self-determination, and advocate homosexual freedom. But I am going to work on it—or, more precisely—toward that transformation. Not because I am given to fits of wild fancy, but because I believe that acts of shared imagination can help unsettle the apocalyptic mindset and can rechannel millennialist desire for a perfected world into viable efforts to make everday life better. The importance of a work like *Angels in America* is that it unfixes absolutes by presenting forms of knowledge that disrupt certainty, a citizenry that dismembers the heterosexist body politic, and love as a force against moral tyranny. Through these breaches in the apocalyptic social standard, hope can emerge.

The future belongs to the impure. The future
belongs to those who are ready to take in a bit
of the other, as well as being what they themselves
are.
   —Stuart Hall, *"Subjects in History: Making Diasporic Identities"*

6 FEELING JEZEBEL: EXPOSING APOCALYPTIC GENDER PANIC AND OTHER CON GAMES

I have always admired the brazenness of celebrating April 1 as an official day for fools and foolery, but at no point in my memory was it ever so aptly timed as April Fool's Day, 1997. Its arrival culminated a week in which nights were spent searching for New Age meanings foretold by comet Hale-Bopp's luminous tail, while mornings brought the latest news about the Heaven's Gate mass suicide. As if this weren't enough, Easter also vied for attention. On one especially unreflective CNN morning newscast, I recall watching newscaster Donna Kelly characterize the Mother Ship belief of Heaven's Gate as bizarre. Yet she didn't bat an eye as she segued to footage of a man splattered with simulated blood, straining under the burden of a huge wooden cross as he made his way through the streets of Jerusalem to commemorate a better-known charismatic preacher, one said to ascend to his own heaven's gate almost two millennia ago and in whose name and promise of imminent return far more than thirty-nine have starved, flagellated, and martyred themselves or tortured and slain others.

So April Fool's Day seemed just right as a climax for this particular stretch of strange days.[1] It was the day, after all, so stunningly commemorated by Herman Melville in *The Confidence Man*, to my mind, the darkest skeptical revelation in all of U.S. literature. Melville's portrayal of a day's journey on the *Fidele*, a fictional American ship of fools, exposes the combination of gullible belief and deep distrust that he scathingly diagnosed as the American Way. Many of the various confidence men he placed aboard his metaphorical ship of state were as likely to be self-deceived as deceiving. Some of the most egregious con men aboard the *Fidele* are true believers in their own confidence game and its players, yet wildly suspicious that someone else is trying to pull the wool over their eyes. Well over a century later, the United States seems to have more than its share of confidence men, gullible fools, and mistrustful misanthropes.

Like Melville, I often find this pattern of American fleece and-be-fleeced behavior amusing, in a black-humor sort of way. Which means it is not simply amusing. As he amply demonstrates, the combination of unwarranted suspicion and profound gullibility that keeps recurring in U.S. culture can and does have dire effects, at its worst breeding suffering, hatred, and violence. One of the themes of *The Confidence Man* is that naive credulity combined with conspiratorial mistrust becomes a prime obstacle to democracy. Although I am not disposed to Melville's deep pessimism, which bordered on despair, there are certain combinations of media onslaught and religious zeal that confirm his worst suspicions about American confidence games and their players.

Apocalypse has long been a major confidence game—for over 2,000 years no less. But apocalypticism these days, which is converging with media-hyped millennialism, ranks at the top of my list of dangerous combinations—dangerous to democracy in general and women in particular. I stipulate the effect on women because, to put it bluntly, apocalyptic theology is structured around the subordination of women. And much contemporary media, saturated as it is with apocalyptic conspiracy thinking, forwards its own brand of misogyny—one that might be seen as a post-feminist return of the masculinist repressed. It is not all that surprising, then, that contemporary millennialism, fused as it is with religious righteousness, fervor, and conspiratorial terror is fueling apocalyptic gender panic.

Gender panic is that sense of alarm, consternation, and anger that results from the loss of male authority. It is often accompanied by troubling confusion about one's place and identity *as* a man or *as* a woman. This is not the first time such panic has surfaced. The ends and beginnings of centuries tend to induce strident gender oppositions.[2] Our era has been no exception. Indeed, at the end of one millennium and the beginning of another, the panic has taken on a greater momentum with insistences that it might be a last chance for the "New Era." Of course, there is more than one way to think about changes in the order of things. Since apocalyptic order means masculinist rule, I, for one, welcome some heavy-duty destabilization. Precisely because feminists have made considerable headway in changing the order of male privilege and economic advantage, some men are fighting hard to retain or regain their privilege, filling the years on both sides of the new millennium with heated rhetoric about male leadership and the "proper" submission of women.

Although contemporary gender panic derives from any number of culturally specific sources—ranging from the medical capacity to transform genitals surgically to late-capitalist economic pressures on family groups—it is often expressed in long-standing images and assumptions. One of the longest-lasting icons of gender panic—indeed one that has had notable force for millennia—is the figure of Jezebel. Tina Pippin has strikingly described Jezebel's duration as a kind of "vamp/ire," because she seemingly "cannot be killed" and is "constantly reformed in the image of male desire and fear." Pippin poses a provocative question. Can Jezebel be "re-vamped" for a feminist reading? Rather than answering either way, however, she ends by asking another question: "Is her story continually recolonized, reopened, the brief scenes of her life reenacted and reinscribed?"[3] While the space here won't allow for a full-scale Jezebel genealogy—a daunting but valuable project—I do want to fill in some background about the Bible's two "Jezebels" in order to show how those portrayals still function to recolonize women within contemporary apocalyptic gender panic.

To combat such panicked reinscriptions of Jezebel as a threat to the security of both men and women, I think it is time not only to revamp her but, more crucially, to *revitalize ourselves* in the spirit of Jezebel. Against an ongoing denunciation of certain women as Jezebels, geared as it is to constrain women's sexuality and restrict women's leadership roles, I seek to be and speak and feel a bit more Jezebelian. Skeptical revelation has much to gain from Stuart Hall's insight—which apocalyptic rhetoric so stridently denies—that we benefit from taking in a "bit of the other." To "take in a bit" of Jezebel facilitates a skeptical questioning of our own normative beliefs. Hall also points out the value of people "being what they themselves are." Here I take his words to suggest that, since women are "always already" inscribed as Jezebels, we may be more ready than we know to call a con game when we see it. And I have seen enough evidence in men to think them capable of following suit—if they are willing. Recognizing these Jezebelian inscriptions as a potential force for transformative critique, and thereby rejecting their conditioned impulse for self-denunciation, is an act of skepticism applied to the self. Feeling Jezebel is an aesthetics of self that courts such skepticism and dances on the threshold of revelation.

Here Comes Jezebel, Here Comes Jezebel, Right down Jezebel Lane

"Jezebel" is the name given to the woman teacher denounced by the Book of Revelation as a false prophet. Religious and secular historians generally agree that Jezebel was not her actual name. Calling her Jezebel was a shorthand way to dramatize just how dreadful a sinner she was. It evokes an earlier Jezebel of the Old Testament, told about in 1 and 2 Kings. Although these two Jezebels are very different women with distinct life stories, the use of the label *Jezebel* conflates them under a single name, which, to compound the insult, is not the given name of either one. The Hebrew designation of the name of the first woman called Jezebel is actually a maligning pun made by rendering her given name, which honored Ba'al, to signify 'dung.'⁴ This conflation of the two women under the designation *Jezebel* is significant because it highlights what the two biblical stories have in common, namely, themes of female authority, flesh, and food—and, finally, gruesome punishment. Crucially, both so-called Jezebels came to prominence at a time of intense battle over rival belief systems and dynastic power—not unlike today's clash of values between the theocratic right and secular democratic forces. The only record we have of their respective stories is the one chronicled by their enemies who proved victorious.

Jezebel senior, as it were, was the ninth-century B.C.E. "daughter of Ethbaal, king of the Sidonians" (1 Kings 16:31). According to Israelite teaching, when she married King Ahab of Israel, she became his downfall. As a worshiper of Ba'al, a fertility warrior god, rather than of Yahweh, she brought the threat of competing customs and beliefs into Israel. Far worse than merely refusing to switch allegiance to Yahweh at a time when Yahweh followers were striving to elevate their patron god to supreme God status, she promulgated her own beliefs, influencing her husband to worship Ba'al and supporting—specifically having them eat at her table—hundreds of prophets to spread the word. That Queen Jezebel could afford to feed so many prophets suggests independent means or control over Ahab's wealth.

Food and power and wealth also figure in her relations with her husband. When Ahab is dejected because his power is insufficient to take over a vineyard he desires to add to his land, she encourages him to "Get up, eat some food, and be cheerful." She also acts as if she were King, taking it upon herself to obtain the vineyard for which Ahab longs, which, according to the record, she does by having the owner killed under Ahab's name and seal (1 Kings 21:5–7). At the end, she herself becomes food for dogs. According to the biblical chroniclers, Jezebel had waged fierce battle against their own prophet Elijah, ruthlessly destroying his prophets. In turn, Elijah, acting (of course justifiably) in service of Yahweh, ordered the slaughter of her prophets. He later prophecies her dreadful end, giving a cruel symmetry to the themes of flesh and food: "The dogs will eat Jezebel within the bounds of Jezreel" (1 Kings 21:23).[5] Jezreel is historically significant in the legacy of the first Jezebel because for Christians it links her to the second one. According to the Book of Revelation, Jezreel is the plain where the battle of Armageddon is to occur.

As the first story goes, Ahab shows regret for his deeds and his punishment is deferred to the next generation. Not so for Jezebel. After Ahab's death, Jezebel goes to live in Jezreel. She remains unrepentant, defying Jehu, now king of Israel. It is Jehu who denounces her "whoredoms" and her "sorceries" (2 Kings 9:22). In keeping with his accusations, the story states that just before her confrontation with Jehu, she bedecked herself by painting her eyes and making "beautiful her head" (2 Kings 9:30). So adorned, she taunts him from her window. But her servants, who are eunuchs and thus presumably indifferent to her feminine wiles, betray her, throwing her down at Jehu's command. And Elijah's words come to pass. Her body is trampled by passing horses, "her blood spattered on the wall" (9:33), and almost all of her body is consumed by dogs. Her skull, her feet, and the palms of her hands remain. The theme of consumption continues: upon witnessing this scene, Jehu "went in and he ate and he drank" (9:33–34).

For a member of the Jesus sect such as John of Patmos, calling a woman *Jezebel* carried a heavy load of venom. Evoking the drama of the name suggests that her transgressions are murderous—even when they are not about power over life and death at all, but, rather, those other sites of cultural contestation, such as sexuality, food, and wealth. By doing so, John also dignifies himself as part of the prophetic lineage of Elijah, who was rewarded by being "taken up by whirlwind into heaven" (2 Kings 2:1). Both are thus seen as righteous men who must contend with notorious women—at least according to the versions that have won out. As part of his vision, John records the Son of God commending the church at Thyatira for its "works and charity" but nonetheless admonishing it for tolerating "the woman Jezebel." He is specific about what he deems her wrongdoings, which again entail a woman's expression of power through leadership, sexuality, and food: calling herself a "prophetess," she has endorsed "fornication" and allowed consumption of meats used for sacrificial purposes (Revelation 2:20). Biblical scholars indicate that it is not altogether clear whether she actually preached sexual freedom or if that was simply a way to discredit her in keeping with Jehu's denunciations of her predecessor. In regard to the practice of eating sacrificial meats, this was actually a point of debate in the early church and apparently even Paul allowed it and may have been the one who condoned it in that area when he was founding churches there.[6] Jezebel advocated it, like the Nicolaitans who are also denounced in Revelation, whereas John adhered to the stricter dietary law. Eventually it became a moot point when Christianity no longer used the sacrifice of animals as part of its ritual.

A Cover Story

Other than John's denunciation, virtually nothing is known about the actual woman in question in the Book of Revelation, except that, like her namesake, she taught a contending belief system. Examination of

Revelation, however, does tell us a great deal about what it means to be called a *Jezebel*, in the time that is was written and in the present. In the contemporary United States, the name *Jezebel* is more than ever a conflation of the two different biblical stories because it has come to signify a calculating and murderous woman whose defeat carries apocalyptic urgency. Revelation now serves as a prominent version of what Wahneemah Lubiano calls "cover stories," narratives that "simultaneously mask and reveal political power and its manipulations."[7] Such links between apocalyptic belief and masculinist or male-supremacist conviction are forged throughout Revelation, which has made a grand comeback at the turn of the millennium. Both misogyny and militaristic ideals are covered over and endorsed in the story of the end of time. This is most clear in the way Christian fundamentalists invoke Revelation even as they insist on their devotion to women and that being warriors for God will bring ultimate peace and harmony. It is also what allows secular culture to underwrite blatant misogyny in its borrowings from Revelation for everything from comic books, rock music, films, and television to corporate takeovers and war strategies.

The main point I want to stress is that Revelation depicts paradigmatic apocalyptic gender panic and justifies punishment of and violence against "transgressive" women as necessary for fulfilling God's plan for heaven on earth. I should point out as well that exposing the sexual and gender politics of Revelation hardly excuses or exempts women per se. Many women, in fact, have been key players in the confidence game, carriers of Revelation's vision, tellers of Revelation's cover story, and others have simply complied with its tenets of male dominance and female submission.[8] But women's assent to views that go against their democratic interests does not make the views any less misogynistic. It does suggest that conceding an era of "post" feminism is premature. Instead, feminism needs to be bolstered by bringing skepticism to bear when analyzing women's experience, since it embodies dominant cultural beliefs as well as resistances to the norm.

The goal of Jezebelian skepticism is to expose publically, boldly, and clearly how such misogynistic views are made legitimate. Feminist skeptical revelation makes manifest the myriad ways that these views are given the authority of the law in its full range as divine law, societal law, and psychological norm, which makes them seem natural.[9] Such revelations debunk this authority and show how violence is used to preserve it, how masculinist rule is made compelling by instilling fear of eternal punishment and rousing hope for eternal reward, how these deferred eternities are reinforced by more immediate threats of earthly punishment to women gone awry and earthly promises to honor the "good women," the anti-Jezebels. In the face of rising expectations and efforts for the defeat of nonsubmissive women as promised in Revelation, the time has come for feminist reinvigoration in the spirit of Jezebel.

Exactly what does the cover story of Revelation have to say about what it means to be a woman? Very little actually, and that is part of the problem. Jezebel is the only flesh-and-blood woman to appear in Revelation. All the godly women turn out to be idealized feminine figures. According to Revelation, then, to be a "natural" woman is to be a Jezebel, a descendant of Eve who carries forward her transgressive nature. Therefore, to be a good woman means to have transcended the female body. The "natural" woman pays a high price for her freedom. The vengeful wrath of divine judgment against the Jezebel of Revelation is succinctly stated. John records the Son of God's voice as saying that since Jezebel has refused to repent, she must be punished: "Behold I will cast her into a bed, and them that commit adultery with her into great tribulation, except they repent of their deeds. And I will kill her children with death" (Revelation 2:22–23). Jezebel is thus punished through her body, first through a scene of gang rape that she is said to invite and for which the men may be forgiven if they repent their act, and then through her procreative body with the death of her children, justified presumably because they were conceived of, by, and for her transgression.

The violence against Jezebelian figures does not end there. The story of the Whore of Babylon further encodes misogynistic belief for the sake of establishing moral and civic authority. The metaphor of the city of Babylon as a demonic feminine figure embodying sexual debauchery and commercial corruption again equates being female with being an impure and insatiable temptress and thus a threat to male purity. Once again, sexuality and food are turned against the offender, thus conflating the label *Jezebel* further with the Babylonian enemy. Babylon's punishment is to be made "desolate and naked," to have her flesh eaten and

Albrecht Dürer, *The Whore of Babylon.* Woodcut from The Revelation of St. John. Bibliotheque Nationale, Paris, France. (Giraudon/Art Resource, NY.)

then burned (Revelation 17:16). In this case, wholesale slaughter against both men and women is justified by imaging the imperial city as a depraved and cruel female.

To modern ears, to mine at least, all this vengeance comes across as overkill, literally in the case of Jezebel's children. But it is not unthinkable. In fact, it remains all too familiar in a world in which men's threats of revenge against a woman or women in general often take on sexual expression and encompass children. As we have seen most recently in Bosnia, atrocities of rape and torture occur with enough horrifying regularity in apocalyptically framed warfare to suggest that this passage tacitly serves as a model for their justification, again, in the name of defeating the enemy of truth and righteousness. And such threats are a telling reminder of one of the means by which some men still maintain dominance within their homes.

Just as threats to male rule and Christian religious authority are equated with women's sexual agency, so too purity is gauged by distance from female sexuality. In apocalyptic cover stories, purity is depicted as necessary to preserve the two God-ordained hierarchies which, one, privilege men over women and, two, elevate all true followers over unbelievers. In the Book of Revelation, we see the celebration of this dual status enacted through the 144,000 men who "follow the Lamb" and who *because* they are not "defiled with women" are ushered into the New Jerusalem (14:3–4). The honor of entering into the transformed Holy City, which is adorned as the Bride of Christ, follows a metaphorical logic in which the feminine figure is given in reward to a collectivity of men. The New Jerusalem is of course cast in terms of the most ideal feminine purity and beauty—but such idealization is part of the problem because it is built around a basic gender inequity which presents no attainable reward for flesh and blood women. The text specifies the reward actual men receive but omits any mention of actual women believers; even the possibility of women's spirituality is ignored.

The logic is thus that femininity can only be pure if it is purely metaphysical, as with the Bride. By this criterion, all women are deemed impure by nature. This holds as well for the only other female figure in Revelation, the Woman Clothed with the Sun (Rev 12). It is only when she departs from nature through divine intervention that she stands a chance for survival. As Tina Pippin has pointed out, she is cast in a positive light, since she is favored by God to bear the savior, but in contrast to the other female figures, she "has no name. Her fate is undetermined (although we assume she is safe), whereas the fate of the others is explicitly stated. She is set against a formidable foe, the great red dragon, but with help (from God), she is able to escape. She is speechless except for her cries of pain in childbirth. And she is overlooked—barely visible— since traditionally the battle between God and Satan has overshadowed her importance in the text." Scholars have argued that the Woman Clothed with the Sun probably carries traces of earlier goddess worship, but is reinscribed in Revelation as a submissive figure—one whose submissiveness is her virtue. This is what entitles her to be the virginal mother of the messiah figure, to give birth to the one who will "rule with an iron rod."[10]

Now the Book of Revelation gives us the canonical view of the Apocalypse. In the United States these days, its extremes of violence and virility are not generally deemed acceptable—at least not in "polite company." Nevertheless, a sizeable portion of the population does adhere quite literally to its wrathful morality and prophecy of the End. A 1994 *U.S. News and World Report* poll indicated that just over 60 percent of Americans accept that Jesus will return and that there will be a final judgment day. Somewhat fewer but still significant percentages believe in the Antichrist (49 percent) and the rapture (44 percent).[11] As far as I know, no one asked whether they thought Jezebel's punishment was justified. Numbers for the more extreme Christian Reconstruction movement are smaller (and less known), but their answer would be "yes," since they argue that adulterers and homosexuals should be executed. Thankfully, theirs is not a majority view in the United States; yet they too have made an impact on U.S. policy and life, as can be seen through the work of Randall Terry in particular.[12]

One reason why apocalyptic apprehension and desire are so deeply entrenched in the United States is that televangelism and Internet ministries have a unique capacity to spread Revelation's combination of feverish anxiety and hope by appealing to nationalistic and masculinist moral absolutism. It is important not to mince words here. These men preach hate—in the name of love of the divine. Justifying hatred is en-

Albrecht Dürer, *The Woman Illuminated by the Sun and the Dragon with Seven Heads*. Bibliotheque Nationale, Paris, France. (Giraudon/Art Resource, NY.)

demic to Gerald Flurry's Sunday morning television explications of current global politics as part of the "End time." So too it is in ample evidence in the videos of Jerry Falwell's lecture sermons at Liberty University on how the elect will be able to dominate the unsaved for the thousand-year reign. Evangelical ministries employ the name of Jezebel as a way of warning their congregations about sexual sin and women's usurping of male authority in particular. As Jonas Clark of the Spirit of Life Ministries puts it: "Jezebel is like a shark; she is most vicious and dangerous."[13] And in the words of one evangelical writer on his personal website called "A Prophet's Chamber," the "Jezebelian man" (his term) suffers from "some form of sexual addiction (pornography, perversion, fantasy, etc.)" and "easily yields leadership role to a 'nurturing' female figure (wife, mother or girlfriend)."[14]

The ways in which the secular entertainment and news media aggravate a societal disposition toward apocalyptic fitfulness further extends and heightens gender panic. Even in noncanonical form, the basic gender logic of apocalypticism remains the same, upholding a hierarchy of male authority and female submission, a demonization of women's independence, and a justification of punishment for activities that are deemed impure. These strictures—and the universe of fear, guilt, shame and hatred they inspire—are major components of contemporary apocalyptic gender panic. Their input ranges from grocery store tabloids like the *Sun*, trumpeting that the world will end next week, to prime-time television hype of the phenomenon called millennium fever. Just as apocalyptic belief is dangerous to women, so too millennialism exacerbates this danger, creating possibilities of full-blown gender panic. In keeping with Revelation, women are cast as potential saviors or destroyers, the burden of the world's salvation swinging like a pendulum poised between their rectitude or immorality.

It is not surprising that gender panic erupts full force in concert with "the Millennium." Millennialism in general spurs panic. Rather than learning how to "take in a bit of the other," as Stuart Hall advocates, millennialism breeds fear of a takeover by the other. Millennialist panic is a key ingredient of conspiracy theories that explain current events as a plot by the new world order, the illuminati, or alien invaders. Sometimes the "other" is not conspiratorial so much as simply indifferent to human life. That is apparent in the outbreak of television shows pondering whether the earth will be destroyed by asteroids, earthquakes, viruses, or volcanoes. Such panic is symptomatic of a loss of control and dread of violation. It fights back by overtaking what it sees as the enemy, by turning fear into glorious victory over the other from without and the other of vulnerability within the self.

Millennialism, more specifically, is the fulfillment of *masculinist* (not male) desire. The Book of Revelation again provides the paradigm cover story. For after the horrific blood-soaked imagery of suffering—from plagues, earthquakes, deadly waters, boils, locusts, warmongers, satanic beasts, and from one's own possible impurity—comes the riveting promise: "And God shall wipe away all tears from their eyes, and there shall be no more death, neither sorrow, nor crying, neither shall there be any more pain" (21:4). The ultimate defeat of need, suffering, and death is a second birth achieved without a female body, freed of the obligation of bodily care for others, and relieved of our most profound uncertainty. Any perceived obstacle to this longed-for escape from life is geared to incite panic and possibly violence. Consequently—since millennialism's roots are so deeply mired in a desire to subdue, defeat, and supplant women—this panic, whatever its myriad sources, is already scripted to scapegoat certain women.

Jezebel Now

There is no shortage of Jezebels today. Like the Jezebels of the Bible stories, today's Jezebels are women who challenge the leadership of men, who refuse to be submissive, who teach non-normative systems of belief, who celebrate sexual pleasure. Given the millennialist climate of the United States, it is likely for such women to be condemned by apocalypticists as sluts or femi-nazis—as Jezebels. The con men will continue to restrict women precisely by sexualizing them and then condemning them for their sexuality. Such sexualized gender oppression intersects with racism and classism. As Patricia Hill Collins has shown, the sexualization of black women as Jezebels has particular force in U.S. history, dating back to the days of slavery when white slaveowners blamed the slave women they raped as seducers. She draws on a passage from Lorraine Hansberry's *To Be Young, Gifted and Black* to make it clear how this nexus of sexual exploitation and commodification of women's bodies continues in the stereotype of African American women as prostitutes. Hansberry's character puts it this way: "In these streets out there, any little white boy from Long Island or Westchester sees me and leans out of his car and yells—'Hey there, *hot chocolate*! Say there, Jezebel! Hey you—"hundred dollar misunderstanding"! YOU! Bet you know where there is a good time tonight.'"[15] Presented so starkly here is how a woman of color is disparaged through a racialized sexuality cast as *her* self-prostitution.

These links between race, class, gender, and sexuality gain more force by the simultaneous desexualization of the not-Jezebel, the pure and proper woman. With a millennialist movement like the Promise Keepers, when a woman is not pure—that is, submissive to the apocalyptic order of morality and the confidence men who spread the word—she too is a Jezebel. Indeed, on their logic, to be a feminist is to be a Jezebel. The idea that a Jezebel will bring others "down" to her flesh-loving level is one reason that so much apocalyptic anger and blame gets vented toward feminists. This can even happen within feminism, as splits over pornography, lesbianism, and the status of sex workers indicate. What can also happen with amazing rapidity in these days of accelerated media contact is a complete shift in regard to a particular woman's reputation. Within a week after her death, Diana, Princess of Wales, went from near Jezebel status to an apotheosis as Queen of Hearts, a symbolic link to the Woman Clothed with the Sun. The Diana to be remembered was not the woman with eating disorders and sexual passion but the mother of the son who will reign as king.

Fear of being thought a Jezebel is enough to make some women join the confidence game outright. Such is the case with the various Christian women groups that have organized as counterparts to the Promise Keepers—Promise Reapers, Heritage Keepers, Suitable Helpers, Chosen Women, Women of Promise, and Women of Faith.[16] A secular instance of this is the dating advice book for women called *The Rules: Time-Tested Secrets for Capturing the Heart of Mr. Right*. In this paperback best-seller, co-authors Ellen Fein and Sherrie Schneider preach to their readers such pearls of wisdom as "Rule 17: Let Him Take the Lead" or

"Rule 20: Be Honest but Mysterious." The authors go so far as to promise women that following the rules will not only bring a man to the altar but actually cut down on his infidelity or abuse since he will be "so crazy about you." The book is in many ways merely insipid. This sort of naivete, however, may well be unconscionable, since incidences of domestic abuse are not necessarily correlated with attitudes of diminished fascination.

The popularity of a book such as *The Rules*—and its sequel *Rules II*— is an indicator of gender panic in so far as it is a call to order, an effort to alleviate, even as it fosters, fears of loneliness by reordering heterosexual life around masculine prerogative and just enough feminine wiles to get a girl safely married. Over all, *The Rules* and "Rules Girls," the related self-help groups that have popped up around the country, are fairly innocuous but popular enough to suggest that a good number of turn-of-the-millennium career women are striving to relieve their gender panic with 1950s-style feminine mystique.[17]

What the popularity of *The Rules* makes clear is that gender panic can hit men and women equally. But it also shows that simply trying to calm the panic won't bring women's equality. Apocalyptic thinking and millennialist momentum can only see one way to mollify gender panic: by resurrecting men's authority over women. Sometimes the resurrected voice of masculinist authority is most seductive when it is soft. As Promise Keepers have learned, the language of men's failure to be devoted to women and children is a compelling way to regain authority in the home. Whether the language is soft or hard, it has the same message: Only male authority can save the day. This is explicit in religious apocalypse, but it is also an implicit message of secular apocalypse.

A prime example of secular apocalypse is the television show *Millennium* on FOX. Every week, a sorrowful-faced, automaton-voiced, extra-governmental special investigator named Frank Black journeys into a dark world of biblical-inspired torture and murder. As a psychic semiotician of apocalyptic signs, he then solves the crime and brings peace— albeit temporarily, since it is the show's premise that there are a lot of maniacs out there. To generate panic, *Millennium* typically targets America's mythical safe place—the suburban neighborhood where decent families bring up happy children. One episode, for example, takes place in a planned community called Vista Verdes Estates, where a man is abducting, torturing, and killing teenage boys.[18] The community, it turns out, has locked the menace within its own gates. The killer's pathology is to make the boys drink blood that he has stored in packets in a picnic box. Frank, of course, solves the case, which revolves around the biblical theme of the father's sin visiting itself on his son. The sin in this case was infidelity, which shifts blame to the Jezebel who tempted him. The father who repents his deed is the one whose son is saved.

Critics have complained that the show is buried in futility, but skeptical analysis suggests that, like the Book of Revelation, it dwells on the dark days in order to uphold the combat myth that Norman Cohn has identified as integral to apocalyptic representation.[19] From a skeptical view, Frank Black is a messiah figure, or at least a harbinger of the real thing. *Millennium* strives to capture its audience's attention by instilling a sense of personal helplessness and producing a kind of low-grade panic that curbs any sense of individual agency while activating readiness for order to be restored. Frank Black represents the hopes of ordinary men and women that this helplessness can be defeated—not by their own doing, of course, but by his. Throughout the drama, the hero remains supremely and explicitly committed to that notorious con game known as "family values" which emerged in the Reagan era and remains a buzzword to mark the new millennium. Through masculine insight, supernaturally enhanced by his mysterious "gift" of psychic power, Frank Black becomes a postmodern purveyor of doom and prophet of salvation. It is only by reinstituting his decidedly male authority that apocalyptic gender panic is calmed, allowing father-led families to remain in tact.

Such popular-culture examples provide a vivid backdrop for social policy practices which constitute an assault on sexual freedom and freedom of speech. Within that domain, there are overt efforts to uphold family values by holding down Jezebels. Who are the Jezebels said to threaten the very fabric of the family and the nation? According to the apocalyptic confidence game, there are whole categories of suspect Jezebels who are responsible for societal decline in the form of sexually active teenage girls and women, welfare mothers, sex workers, and lipstick-and-leather lesbians. Public leaders also take the heat of the modern-day Jezebel. They include women like Jocelyn Elders, who was fired as Surgeon General for speaking frankly about safe sex and masturbation. Sexperts like Susie Bright, whose campus lectures on sexual freedom and abortion rights have been denounced as akin to the Holocaust, are also suspect.[20] Performance, visual, and literary artists whose representations of women's untrussed bodies and sexuality have been condemned by congressional con men. In other words, any woman who serves up food for nonapocalyptic thought. These are the Jezebels who are used rhetorically by the Christian Right to stir up gender panic, precisely in order to reinstate apocalyptic order.

Is it possible to stave off gender panic? That remains to be seen. My hunch is that apocalyptically inspired male violence and attempts at dominance will heighten and spread over the next decade. After all, some men really seem to have their hearts set on the thousand-year reign promised in Revelation, during which the Son will "rule with an iron rod." Of course a hunch does not claim the same authority as an apocalyptic revelation (and frankly I'd like to be as colossally wrong as John of Patmos when he predicted that the End was near). It is also possible to claim—create anew—what it means to be a Jezebel on behalf of women's freedom. In this regard, the Jezebel ur-texts got one thing right: women's freedom does revolve around female authority, flesh, and food. These have long been and still are critical sites of gendered power relations, crucial arenas of power through which women's practices of freedom can be either thwarted or manifest.

I want to be clear on this. It is the very thought and practice of women's freedom that generates apocalyptic gender panic. To my mind, such panic is best met head-on in recommitment to feminist principles, especially if those principles are Jezebelian in spirit. Jezebelian skepticism and activism fortify a feminist aesthetics of self that can help stave off and withstand apocalyptic gender panic. Skepticism about the con games of apocalyptic threat and millennialist hope may not be as miraculous as feeding scores with a handful of fish but it can score a fishy story about the menace of feminism. Just as feminism withstood a comparable backlash at the end of the last century to make a difference in this one, it is possible for social transformation in the third millennium to bear the mark, not of the beast, but of Jezebel.

ADDENDUM
CIRCUITS OF REVELATION

(An)other Story

Weird things can happen, even to skeptics. While I was writing
and thinking about Jezebel, I often tried to conjure her up, wondering
about her appearance, her dress, the power of her voice, and the manner
of her preaching—trying to take in a bit of the other. Part of the problem was that there was so little reliable information to go on. Trying to
picture the setting of the early church where she preached proved
equally difficult. Not much historical information is provided on Thyatira. Even the tourist industry treats it as a second-class citizen. Regarding the Seven Ancient Churches package, the Pacha tour book says only
that "Thyatira is the least important of the seven churches."[1] That's not
true for me and it is not clear from Revelation either since, according to
John, when the son of God spoke about Thyatira, his eyes were described as "like unto a flame of fire," hardly an indifferent reaction.

I had almost given up on pondering what Jezebel could offer a skeptic like me, when, lo and behold, as visionaries say, "Jezebel" suddenly
materialized. It all started when I was struggling to learn my new Internet system. Was it a vision? A hallucination? The effect of an over-
wrought imagination? A bit of undigested swordfish? Internet gone hay-
wire? Well, I'm not sure. I compared it to John's account but there were
several differences. John had one spectacular, explosive vision, but I, my

word, . . . I had multiple visitations. And unlike the Son of Man in Revelation, my Jezebel never claimed to have the whole story or that she was the end all and be all. Indeed, what is most clear from bits and pieces of information I received from her on the Net is that there is so much more for lots and lots of Jezebelian women to say and do. And unlike John's cave experience on the isle of Patmos, my visions were a little more hit and miss, randomly taking place in what some might call the Sodom and Gomorrah of the United States, New York City, and the District of Columbia. A few arrived in Geneva, New York, where I teach, making me wonder whether it has become a modern-day Babylon—probably just wishful thinking.

Like John, I have faithfully recorded—in my case, printed out—my visions. Some of them entailed images. I readily admit it, it is daunting trying to render visuals into words. Of course, John had that problem too. Happily, like John, at least the John according to Greek Orthodoxy who was assisted by Prochorus, I was helped along by a modern-day scribe, a student assistant named Rene de Gironemo, whose gathering of some materials on the biblical Jezebels allowed me to grasp some of the finer points and fill in a few blanks on occasion. Fortunately, also, I could download the Internet materials. (John should have been so lucky.) Every now and then, I had to borrow lines from other sources, including John's, to clarify an ambiguous phrase or image. But there is clear historical evidence that John did this too, even though he didn't admit that either. Not that there is anything wrong with it, as Seinfeld and company say about being gay. Such borrowings were apparently as common for prophets and apocalypticists in his day as they are now for postmodern novelists. Despite all these caveats, I am confident that it is every bit as reliable as John's book.

I have called my vision "Circuits of Revelation" and present it here as an Addendum to "Feeling Jezebel." Seeing it in print suggests an experimental poetic form. I particularly like that because I have always said that I could not write a poem to save my life. Perhaps Jezebel's way of blurring lines of discourse, especially the poetic and the technological, is an act of rescue. What does it mean? Reader, I hope you will tell me. That is, link up with Jezebel yourself and turn this visionary supplement into an intercourse of Jezebelian proportions.

Elena Ciletti, *Asparagus Spears I*. Used with permission.

Circuits of Revelation

USERNAME: Quinby
PASSWORD: Skeptic

Chapter 1

Lycos
Search Results
[ISMAP]-[USEMAP]
[ISMAP]-Lycos Services

Companies online . . . We'll Do The Digging For You.
Brought to you by Lycos and D&B.

You Searched [The Web _____] for [all the words _____]
JEZEBEL _____
[LINK] [IMAGE]-Submit
Get more on JEZEBEL. Choose from categories below.

Chapter 2

The revelation which came to skepticism's enthusiast, called Lee, in a phantasmogorical scene materialized on the sixth day of the sixth month through the sixth node of the internet. Lee was wired. The virtual message arose before her on the talking screen, calling out her name and saying unto her: 2 "Send forth a message unto the seven faculties of the pleasures of civilization: the rule busters, the promise breakers, dykes with attitude, the bitches, the witches, the shrews, and the archangels of feminist design." 3 And Lee turned to see the voice that spake with her. And being turned she saw seven golden candlesticks, and in the midst of the seven candlesticks the Amazonian force took shape.   4 Clothed in red-hot leather, this was a vision to behold. Her eyes glistened with the virtual violet glow of new-age electronics, her right hand held seven chips, and out of her mouth came a sharp double-edged critique.   5 And Jezebel sayeth to Lee, "Seal not the sayings of the prophecy of this book for the time is at hand: party on, in and through the body.   6 Send forth your emissaries bearing the good news. They shall conga to the future, saying unto all, 'I heard it though the grapevine, technobody wanna be mine, oh, oh oh.'"²

Chapter 3

[yahoo   l   Write Us   l   Add URL   l   Info]

Topic: Society and Culture: Families

_____ SearchOptions

(*) Search all of Yahoo   ( ) Search only in Families

*Family Planet Headlines   [*]—current news, advice columns and feature articles

Yahoo! Net Events: Families—today's chats and programs.

Adoptions
Childfree
Children
Divorce
Domestic Violence@ (NORMAL LINK) Use right-arrow to activate.

Chapter 4

And this self-same voice came unto me, calling herself Jezebel, but now
her words turned somber and the screen filled with darkness and I
heard shrieks of agony and soft cries.

[INLINE]
Let's Stop Domestic Violence and Child Abuse
It Breaks Homes—It Breaks Hearts—It Breaks Lives

Please help us keep our facts and statistics up to date. If you have any
information that can be posted on these pages (including sources)
please send it to us at: comments @famvi.com

Some Facts (excerpts)

- Domestic Violence is the leading cause of injury to women between
  ages 15 and 44 in the United States—more than car accidents, mug-
  gings, and rapes combined. (Uniform Crime Reports, Federal Bureau
  of Investigation, 1991)
- Battered women are more likely to suffer miscarriages and to give
  birth to babies with low birth weights. (Surgeon General, United
  States, 1992)
- Nearly 2 in 3 female victims of violence were related to or knew their
  attacker. (Ronet Bachman Ph.D., U.S. Department of Justice Bureau
  of Justice Statistics, "Violence Against Women: A National Crime Vic-
  timization Survey Report," January 1994, p. iii)

Chapter 5

[INLINE]
Webcrawler

copyright—1997 Excite, Inc.
[ISMAP]—Excite Search Results

Excite Me: Make It My Web   Power Searching Made Simple

Apocalyptic Confidence Men_____Search Help

99% Confidence Men of America and the Games They Play
URL: http://www.fleece.com.net

Summary:

Bill Bright, Campus Crusades
Jerry Falwell, Liberty University
Bill McCartney, Promise Keepers
Ralph Reed, Christian Right Pundit/Consultant
Pat Robertson, American Center for Law and Justice
Rousas John Rushdoony, *Institutes of Biblical Law*
Randall Terry, Operation Rescue

Love, Jezebel

© Copyright 1997 Excite Inc. Disclaimer

Chapter 6

dialing vax
atdt 666-*666

[LINK]
Click here to see our pic

1 When the clown shall make of his balloons omegas instead of dachs-
   hunds, when the Piltdown man shall rag his sleeve and the plenum
   hitch up its sans-a-belt pants with the silver cord,
2 then shall we peek out of the underwear drawer of time as the night
   will out of its 2,000 eyes, and witness the coming.
3 Cometary and brilliant, then, will appear the Sapphos and the
   Sophias of our wonder and each will spell their name with the *J* of
   Jill of all Trades, the *E* of *Embrasure*, the *Z* of *Zest of Zeal*, the second
   E of *Emendation*, the *B* of *Braided Blasphemy*, the third *E* of *Empow-
   ering Emporium*, and the *L* of *Liquid Fire*.
4 And these Jezebels will bestride the tremendous clitoral equinox that
   shall bid farewell to the tubular lunacies of our patristic age,

Elena Ciletti, *Asparagus Spears II.* Used with permission.

5 and embrace a menu of merry myths steaming with a new pungency.
6 It shall be Jezebel who enunciates at last the tetragrammaton that
   will silence the manifold senilities of our present-day evangelisms.
7 Look to your own: strip down, rouge up, buy your outfit of choice,
   but do it now. The time has come. Carry On!³

7 Programmed Perfection, Technoppression, and Cyborg Flesh

As the millennium turns, the desire to deify or demonize technology seems to be getting harder to resist. Resistance to apocalyptic fervor is prudent, however. Myths of technological deliverance or perdition seldom yield tenable political and ethical judgments. Nevertheless, the fact that more and more people qualify to be called cybernetic organisms, or cyborgs, has surely exacerbated the momentum of apocalyptic fear and millennial hope.[1] We can witness this heightened expectation readily enough in the Heaven's Gate suicides and the ensuing media furor over the role the Internet played in the group's decision. But cultural theory has also been swept up in technological millennialism. As evidence of just how difficult it is to withstand these impulses, let me cite two leading analysts of technology whose writings explicitly castigate apocalypticism.

For over a decade now, Donna Haraway's Cyborg Manifesto has been a guiding light in feminism and cultural studies.[2] It may seem unfair to criticize her "ironic political myth" as apocalyptic when she explicitly declares its distance from apocalypse. The problem is that she also claims apocalyptic drama for her cyborg figure. Apart from her contradicting statement that "the cyborg is also the awful apocalyptic *telos* of the 'West's' escalating dominations of abstract individuation,"[3] I am concerned that she flattens out cyborg subjectivity into *the* cyborg. This facilitates a full-scale slide from metaphor to ontology. Such mythologizing not only maintains an apocalyptic tone but also produces apocalyptic Truth, precisely what Haraway seeks to combat.[4] Her utopian pronouncement that "By the late twentieth century, our time, a mythic time, we are all chimeras, theorized and fabricated hybrids of machine and organism; in short, we are cyborgs" is located well within, not, as she would have it, "outside salvation history."[5]

The encroachment of apocalypticism continues in Haraway's recent book, again despite an expressed antiapocalyptic stance which is foregrounded in the figure of the "modest witness." This too derives from a mythologizing of cyborgian existence—as if all cyborgs were the same and all hypertext formations cast a single shadow. The problem is that the cyborg as initially conceptualized is a mythology that now resists attempts at empiricizing it.[6] Indeed, that is what gives it so much force. But that mythical force, in turn, renders less plausible her proposal that a "liveable worldwide web should be the mutated modest witness's game of cat's cradle, where the end of the millennium becomes a trope for swerving away from the brands that mark us all in the too persuasive stories of the New World Order, Inc."[7] The concept of the cyborg is too steeped in the myth of the millennium as a New World Order to combat it.

Similarly, though in a dystopian vein, Paul Virilio's critique of religious apocalypticism slips into a form of apocalyptic cultural critique when he envisions the technological horizon: "The will to power of a science without a conscience will pave the way for a kind of intolerance yet unimaginable today precisely insofar as it will not simply attack certain peculiarities of the species, like sex, race, or religion. It will attack what is alive, 'natural' vitality finally being eliminated by the quasi-messianic coming of wholly *hyperactivated* man."[8] This ten-year trajectory from *the* cyborg to *the* cyborg overman registers the degree of millennial fever within cultural theory. Virilio's critique partakes of yet another feature inherent to apocalyptic rhetoric, the demonization of the Other. Distinctions between criticism and demonization are well worth keeping in mind. Again, as with mythologizing, demonization flattens out what needs to be detailed in, losing sight of specific agents, actions, and consequences of technology.

Whether salvific or catastrophic, apocalyptic rhetoric about technology is exhilarating and persuasive because it triggers deeply entrenched desires for the millennialist dream: transcendence of human limitations. The technological avatar of transcendence is often excess. Both Haraway and Virilio employ the idea of excess in their respective theorizations, though in opposite ways, Haraway as a means of challenging dualisms and hierarchy and Virilio as the threat inherent in what he calls "Technoscientific Fundamentalism." By definition, of course, cyborgs do exceed bodily limitation. But it does not follow that excess in and of itself constitutes either a democratic political strategy or a tyrannical assault on life. Again, part of the problem is the way that excess is being either deified or demonized: in Haraway's manifesto, mythologizing excess as a subversive element renders it deficient as a political strategy; in Virilio's case, it is both the enemy to be warded off and the already overdetermined future, which also leaves no room for political resistance. In other words, apocalyptic-oriented techno-theory tends to be caught in a tangle of humanistic moralizing even while declaring that we are all posthuman.[9]

Given this pull toward crisis-oriented millennialism, is it possible to theorize about the opportunities and obstacles that cyborgian technology poses for democracy without reproducing the terms of apocalyptic discourse? This chapter is an effort to do that, drawing on Foucauldian genealogy as well as both Haraway's and Virilio's descriptions of human and machine interfaces. Despite the reservations expressed above, the nonapocalyptic features of these deservedly influential analyses are vital for understanding conditions of contemporary society and subjectivity.

To provoke thought about cyborgian technology and democratic life and to help amplify an approach to technology that is skeptical rather than apocalyptic, I draw on the 1995 film *Strange Days* (directed by Kathryn Bigelow, Lightstorm Entertainment) and present quotations from the film in the following italicized epigraphs. I have chosen it as a focal point for several reasons. One is that, like much contemporary cultural theory (though for a larger audience), the film combines apocalyptic and nonapocalyptic representations of technology and U.S. society at the turn of the millennium. A second reason is that, with a nod to Nathaniel Hawthorne's "Young Goodman Brown," the film presents itself as a postmodern allegory. Both center on a man who loses faith in a woman named Faith; both speculate on what Hawthorne calls "ocular deception"; and both focus on forces of evil and sexuality. But unlike Hawthorne's ending of gloom and distrust, *Strange Days* is a moralizing tale of love and redemption, an effect, I believe, of utopian longings endemic to apocalypticism. Third, the film's explicit treatment of cyborgian life raises salient questions about technology and subjectivity in postmodern millennial times. And finally, I concur—these are strange days. But we don't have to be apocalyptic about them.

As a skeptical countermove, I read the film as a problemization of what I call "technoppression," an authoritarian configuration of power, truth, and morality that is rapidly gaining in tenacity, intensity, and pervasiveness. Technoppression is *not* synonymous with technology. It is an *apocalyptic use of technology* that veers toward social domination; technoppression operates by engendering utopian hopes while arousing dystopian fears. While my theory of technoppression does not declare this an apocalyptic moment, despite our calendar confirming that "2K IS COMING," it does argue that this is a crucial time for bolstering resistance to antidemocratic forces. I advance this theory in "the day of reckoning" section, but first I want to show some previews.

"It is about the stuff you can't have, the forbidden fruit."
—Lenny Nero

Billed as "a sexy kinetic thriller," *Strange Days* is set in Los Angeles during the final days of this millennium, when "anything is possible," "nothing is forbidden."[10] The film is a hybrid of genres, intertwining mystery, horror, romance, pornography, millennialism, and science fiction. The central device bringing all these together is literally just that, a device of virtual technology: the SQUID receptor, the "super-conducting quantum interference device" that records human experiences onto clips that Lenny Nero (Ralph Fiennes) pushes on the black market.

Viewers are introduced to SQUID by way of an adrenalin-pumping opening scene which positions the camera so that audience members "become" participants in the action. Suddenly, I *am* one of a group of men on the way to a robbery. Once "we"—he and I—enter the crime site, all hell breaks loose. Because of the camera eye's chaotic closeness and the jumble of noise—shouts, pleas for mercy, rapid footsteps, gunshots—the sense of proximity is intense. Just as "we" begin "our" getaway, the police arrive and "we" frenetically race up several flights of stairs to the roof where the only escape is a leap from one building to the next. "We" freeze at the edge, circle back with a curse, and then try the leap. The camera captures "our" hands as "we" fall short of the jump, plunging downward into space. Abruptly, the screen fills with snowy interference. Then cues resituate me. I have been watching a snuff clip with Lenny Nero, seeing what he sees as he experiences the robber's experiences through the SQUID device wired to his skull.

"Faith, call me."

—Lenny Nero

Lenny Nero is his own best customer. His name suggests his initial outlook and moral plight: his existence is black yet he "plays" as L.A. burns; he is also a cross between "zero" and "hero," a former cop with a conscience who was apparently justifiably thrown off the vice squad, now thoroughly demoralized by the corruption he sees all around. He has lost faith in humanity, a disillusionment induced largely because he has lost the woman he loves, Faith Justin (Juliette Lewis). Worse yet, Faith is "lost" because she has become the lover of Philo Gant (Michael Wincott), an allegorically cast evil figure who rules over a world of dark corruption, encapsulated by his nightclub hangout rife with sadomasochistic performance groups. Lenny has little left but the shoebox full of clips from his happier days when he still had Faith. He is hooked on SQUID clips and it's easy enough to see their attraction. In certain ways, SQUID clips are better than dreams, since one can buy the content, and superior to regular memory, because SQUID memory is full-bodied and never fades. Electronic playback gives the same sensations as the actual experience. But the film also highlights SQUID's alienation effect through a doubling back of his image in the mirror, so that on screen we see two images of Lenny reliving his desire for Faith, reexperiencing his pleasure in her body, and yet remaining alone with only his clips.

One of the dangers of a device like SQUID is that daily existence can come to seem like just another copy, as is evident when Lenny awakens in the afternoon to the television announcing the incident that will become the pivotal action of the film. Two rap stars have been murdered in what the L.A.P.D. has declared to be a gangster-related, execution-style killing. Footage shows a close-up of Jeriko One (Glenn Plummer), a black activist and recording star who has recently called for revolution against the racist police state. For Lenny, this is simply more background noise; he has more clips to push. When his new customer, an attorney with "a virgin brain," indicates that he knows that SQUID technology was developed for the feds to replace a body wire, Lenny emphasizes its phenomenological component: "This is life. This is a piece of somebody's life. You're there. You're doing it, seeing it, feeling it." And adds seductively, "I'm your priest, I'm your shrink, I'm your main connection to the switchboard of the soul. I'm the magic man, the Santa Claus of the subconscious."

While Lenny's little speech doesn't yet convince his new customer, it does amusingly confirm a certain trajectory from priest to therapist to electronic capitalist. What does persuade the customer is the experience he has when he lets Lenny wire him. Once the electronic tentacles are hooked up, viewers see his body stir in pleasure. His hands gently caress his chest as his head rolls backward—and then abruptly he's out of it as Lenny switches off the system. He has *been* an eighteen-year-old girl taking a shower. If such a technology were actually to be devised, it could offer some genuine "humanitarian services," the phrase Lenny Nero uses to defend his trade. (Its actualization is hardly out of the question. Places like MIT's Media Lab are at work exploring such linkups.)[11] As with literature and film, being wired means that you don't have to be "there" to get bodily thrills of horror or pleasure. But SQUID offers even more because to "jack in" means that, although you are "not there"—in the way the one whose experience is recorded is—you are in some real sense "there"—because the device sends the recorded signals from the cerebral cortex of the recorder (the word applying to both person and machine) to the one who gets wired. As Lenny says, it lets people experience their dark side without recrimination and sex without risk of disease or death. And as the clip he has just used to make his sale indicates, one could experience a transgendered body without the expense, physical pain, or ostracism involved in transsexual surgery.[12]

Strange Days extends beyond this futuristic interface to highlight a number of pressing issues involving power, truth, and ethics in the present day. It amply demonstrates that the most sophisticated technology exists amidst forces of physical brutality and cultural institutions of disciplinary power. One of its key insights is that, even if we were "all cyborgs," we would not be entirely virtual or hyperreal. This is a useful reminder to cultural theorists like Jean Baudrillard who tend to describe the world in terms of overriding simulation or hyperreality in which "there is no longer any instance of power, any transmitting authority— power is something that circulates and whose source can no longer be located, a cycle in which the positions of dominator and the dominated interchange in an endless reversion which is also the end of power in its classical definition."[13] What I am arguing, by contrast, is that, even with its futuristic device and implausible plot resolution, *Strange Days* more accurately exhibits the complexity of the intertwined power formations operating today.

"The day of reckoning is upon us."
—*Jeriko One*

From a perspective of millennial skepticism, every day is a day to be reckoned with. Such reckoning benefits from the genealogical method outlined by Foucault, which entails three axes of investigation—power relations, truth, and ethics—each of which features an aspect of subject formation. According to Foucault, the power axis examines how "we constitute ourselves as subjects acting on others"; the truth axis explores how we become "subjects of knowledge"; and the ethical axis discerns how "we constitute ourselves as moral agents."[14] Foucault drew on this approach in his various studies, employing it in the *History of Sexuality*, Volume 1, to guide his argument about two primary power/knowledge formations in the West, the system of alliance and the deployment of sexuality.[15] Although the terms of Foucault's formulations are well-known to cultural theorists, I reiterate some of them here in order to locate my concept of technoppression in relation to them and reorient Foucauldian theory in the present. First, I want to underscore Foucault's argument that the deployment of sexuality has *not* replaced that of alliance. As he stated, while the deployment of sexuality "does tend to cover up the deployment of alliance, it has neither obliterated the latter nor rendered it useless."[16]

At the same time, I want to stress that postmodern cultural conditions have also brought about a third form of power relations which I call "programmed perfection." Technoppression is a particularly authoritarian part of this third formation, one that combines with the most intense forces from the other two power formations. For the forces of technoppression, social domination is a goal.[17] My major concern is to emphasize that contemporary American society is subject to and threatened by all three different but intertwined modes of force, all of which involve apocalyptic fulmination about sexuality, making sexuality a primary vehicle for extensions of control in other facets of our lives.

Under the system of alliance (based on relations of kinship), which was consolidated when power was concentrated in the Monarchy and authorized through religious authority, power over others is maintained through physical punishment, including the seizure and imprisonment of bodies, and death. Alliance functions today in its obverse form through rape, gay, lesbian, and transgender bashing, and racial violence. But most of all alliance operates legally. Or to put it more accurately: Law is the framework of alliance. Its moral assumptions of family and kinship divide the natural from the unnatural. Hence certain sexual acts are castigated as unnatural, as with antisodomy laws, for example.

Alliance also operates through quasi-legal means, as with today's common law court movement. Rough estimates for membership in the patriot and militia movements range from 15,000 to 25,000, but their influence is stronger than those numbers, given the way they have used liens on property and the way that some of the extremists have used bombs and arson in the name of a higher law.[18] Smaller groups in the deployment of alliance, like the U.S. Taxpayers Party, are fortified by the more extensive Christian Right effort to establish theocratic rule in the United States.[19] And they, as well as large groups like the Christian Coalition rely heavily on cyberspace communication. That is why a banal group like the Promise Keepers is more troubling than their rah-rah appearance would suggest. They too have an active web-life that spreads their missionary zeal to many other nations.

In short, the deployment of alliance is alive, thriving, and wired. So is the deployment of sexuality, which is dispersed through myriad disciplinary practices, including education, medicine, the family, and social welfare agencies. Its "kinder and gentler" form of demonization declares noncompliance to be perverse: instead of death or imprisonment, this deployment is enforced through secularized confession as a primary mode of self-surveillance and offers therapy as a way to become normal—or at least cope. It is not an exaggeration to say that the United States has become a thoroughly therapeutic society. The reach of disciplinary power also stretches further through technoscience; some chat rooms are little more than sessions of confessional desire.

At the same time, we are in the midst of another formation of power that entails neither punishment nor management, but rather a form of biological mastery that seeks nothing short of perfection. Foucault clearly had inklings of this formation, but he did not theorize it. His vocabulary of networks and dense transfer points derives from computer technology, but the deployment of sexuality really operates through very different forms of surveillance and expertise. I have called the most dominating trajectories of programmed perfection *technoppression* in order to highlight the primary oppressive forces at work in conjunction with technology. As with the other power formations, sexuality is a key relay station for programmed perfection in general and technoppression in particular. Programmed perfection weighs down and circumscribes the great diversity that technology makes possible while pressing flesh into a monolithic container labeled *perfect*. We need to read that label more skeptically to be apprised about the potential danger of this formation. While technology is not in and of itself oppressive, a consolidation of its uses to advance monopoly capitalism, militarism, and heterosexism surely is. Such consolidation is the blunt force of technoppression.

Because programmed perfection has a greater range of power networks than do the deployments of alliance and sexuality, it also has a greater capacity to replace power relations with domination (my use of the term *technoppression* is synonymous with *domination* within this third formation). Like the deployment of sexuality, power relations within programmed perfection are more dispersed than centralized—indeed, far more so, given the rapidity and anonymity of electronic circulation. This is why Baudrillard is right to announce a distinct form of power that circulates without locatable source, though—it is necessary to repeat it—he is off target to see it as the only form of power.[20] More crucially, he gives up the struggle way too soon. Foucault also admitted that "we are perhaps living the end of politics" but insisted that it is therefore "necessary to invent another one or something which could substitute for it."[21] And he, importantly, distinguished between power and domination, indicating that power and freedom are correlative, whereas domination closes down on freedom. Part of the task of cultural analysts and activists, then, is to ensure that technology remains open to transfers of power, without which there is no practice of freedom.[22]

How does programmed perfection conceal its technoppressive maneuvers toward domination? How does it make itself enticing? Rather than distinguishing between the "licit and the illicit" as in alliance, or between the normal and the abnormal as in sexuality, technoppression selects techniques integral to programmed perfection to divide the perfect from the defective. Technoppression advances bodily embellishment as not simply desirable and attainable but also indispensable.[23] The dream of bioperfection conceals the threat of biodomination. Genetic engineering, for example, promises to eradicate malfunctioning genes, but behind that hope lurk arguments for the elimination of everything from fat genes to homosexual ones. A second enticement is a new visibility by way of electronic imagery that transubstantiates bodies, creating new forms of surveillance that are simultaneously internal and external. Implantation devices installed for purposes ranging from monitoring internal organs to tracking specified individuals are justified through an incitement to bioperfection, of either an individual body or of the cultural body politic. Programmed perfection does not just promise that electronic prosthetics will perfect life—it mandates it.[24] And it is the mandate of perfection that we need to be especially skeptical about because these power/knowledge relations can so readily transfer into technoppressive forces of domination.

Technology's ability to alter organic matter brings a significant shift in perception and experience of bodies.[25] Much has been written about the "disappearance" of the body as a result of cyborgian attachment to computer screens or, correlatively, a transcendence of the body through machine replacements. I am arguing, however, that cultural theory should accentuate the obvious: even though the body is altered through communication technologies, it does not disappear into information; nor is it transcended, even when we enter virtual communities. We do not, as cyberpunk terminology would have it, escape our "meat," any more than the self-flagellating, fasting ascetics under the system of alliance transcended their flesh. Indeed, as Nietzsche pointed out, the ascetic is, perhaps more than most, ever aware of the body he or she disdains. So too with virtual subjects, whose bodies, after all, receive the sought-after pleasures of cyber-connection. It is also bodies that are left aching from sitting so long at their terminals or nauseous and disoriented from trips into virtual reality. The desire for final freedom from bodily constraint is a gender-inflected dream with a two thousand-year history, updated March 1997 when the Heaven's Gate members poisoned and suffocated their "containers." From the Book of Revelation to the Heaven's Gate website, denial of embodiment has been a heterosexist obsession that defines itself oppositionally to women's bodily excess and lesbian and gay sexuality.[26]

But it is not inevitable for technology to be a culmination of oppressive values. Indeed, the cyborgian joining of body and machine is forcing a valuable problemization of technology and the millennialist promise of perfection. In this sense, the *cyborg* is to programmed perfection what the *homosexual* is to the deployment of sexuality and what the *sodomite* is to the system of alliance. Each figure is a categorical identity created by its respective power/knowledge formation. As such, its boundaries simultaneously demarcate and cast doubt on what it means to be human within the tenets of each system.[27] We need to keep this intersection of power relations in mind in order to sustain problemization as a counterapocalyptic move.[28] I would also stress that the use of technology makes possible new pleasures, countermemories, and other figures of truth, a process entwined with permutations in power, knowledge, and ethics.

It is probably an exaggeration to say that cyborgian problemization of everyday life is rampant, but it is on the rise. Access to information banks is redefining truth and complicating whether truth can be established amidst an overwhelming flow of data. New imaging techniques further confound assumed correlations between what happens off the screen and what happens on the screen. And programmed perfection's insistence on life enhancement to the point of perfectibility is altering the terms of ethical conduct. Debates about the use of drugs like Prozac, fetal monitoring, cloning, and confidentiality for electronic communication attest to this. Some of the most pointed elements of this debate revolve around death, which serves as the ultimate limit under the deployment of sexuality, but which, under the logic of programmed perfection, promises to be defeated—or at least become a choice.

"It's Real Time. Time to get real, not play back."
—Larette "Mace" Mason

In late-capitalist society—even if it is not quite true that images can kill—it is true that worker production of images and information renders bodily harm and that their consumption has so dramatically altered perceptions of reality that many people suffer disorientation. Within the logic of technoppression, it is impossible to "get real" because of myriad fusions (and hence confusions) between "real time" and "reel time." For *Strange Days*'s character Faith, real life lags behind a perceptual reality formed by movies and playback. "You know one of the ways that movies are still better than playback?" she asks Lenny. "Cause the music comes up, there's credits, and you always know when it is over." Ironically, when "Mace" (Angela Bassett) beseeches Lenny to "get real," a plea that signifies the ethical imperative of the film, the oral delivery retains an undecidability.

While retaining that ambiguity as one of the film's forceful insights, I want to stress that the reality of cyborg flesh is less confusing when approached by way of resistance to the effects of technoppression's power on specific bodies. SQUID serves as a metaphor for a question that accompanies a new generation of video palmcorder users: Are we making videos or are videos making us? From a skeptical genealogical perspective, the question is worded wrongly, since power and resistance go hand-in-hand. Video subjectivity has features of resistance still perhaps best exemplified by the Rodney King video in which "home-made" recordings can bear witness to official brutality. But as the opening scene of *Strange Days* also indicates, producing videos can entail exploitation and risk of injury and death. As with movie production, things can and do go wrong. A stunt double's daredevil act can result in injury; or a staged production can kill or maim real people.

Although I am admittedly pushing to make this correlation, the film can be read to evoke parallel dangers to technology workers in a more widespread and everyday sense. Information technology is particularly notable for its repetitive strain injuries. It is estimated that by "the year 2000, the at-risk figure will rise to 75 percent of all workers."[29] In the service of data omniscience and digital precision, worker bodies under technoppression are chronically injured, with symptoms including radiation exposure, miscarriage, eyestrain, and repetitive strain injuries to muscles and nerves. This bodily consequence is only beginning to be recognized as a feature weighty enough for cultural analysis. But attention to this aspect of technology is a way to avoid utopian or dystopian proclamations about technology and strengthen possibilities for resistance that emerge from within a given power network. As Iain Boal argues, "new conditions of work throw up new sites of resistance—production bottlenecks have always been weak spots, and now 'just-in-time' inventory creates its own particular vulnerabilities. Most machines are abuser friendly"; he adds that, in regard to consumption, "mass boycotts of selected products terrify the personnel in sales and marketing."[30] Although Boal's argument is a valuable extension of Marxist analysis of late-capitalist production, its emphasis on work stoppages does not go far enough.

My theory of technoppression argues that it is time to both get real and get reel—that is, to combine political resistance with the political agency offered by information technology, not only to make demands for bodily protection and health care for cyborg workers but also to make new "reelities."

"I don't need saving. Just give up on me."
—*Faith Justin*

Throughout *Strange Days*, women's exploitation is evinced in a heterosexist propensity for pornographic clips; the film makes this point as both symptom and critique. Its semigraphic sex clips place it on the borderline between now normative R-rated films (the rating of *Strange Days*) and still (ostensibly) non-normative hard-core pornography. For example, the film displays one of Lenny's porno clips, a close-up scene between two women in which one is fondling the silicone-embellished breast of the other. Its showing within the film points out the loss of distinction between mainstream and pornographic sex representation, especially with increasing consumption of video pornography by both men and women and late-night sex channels on television (which are genitally graphic, unlike the clips in *Strange Days*). The debates about the effects of print and cinematic pornography are not close to being resolved (nor do I think they should be if it means ending discussion through censorship) even as the emerging technology of virtual reality complicates them further in two respects. One is that simulation alters the groundwork for the radical feminist critique of the exploitation of women actors in pornographic films. Another is that virtual porn does not have the same status as, for example, a billboard on a public street. It is true that video-conferencing allows pornographic images and words to intrude onto one's computer screen, but it is also possible for viewers to talk back or log off in ways not previously available.

While it remains to be seen whether cybersexuality will replace print, film, and video pornography (an unlikely event any time soon), it is important to understand more fully what the subject effects are—for both men and women on-line—of simulations of sex and sexual violence against women. On-line sex harassment and scenes of rape and torture serve as technoppression's way of reinstituting male dominance. Fortunately, all-male enclaves, or electronic men's clubs, are harder to maintain since women have access to the system. Rather than calling for a cyber vice squad to outlaw sex-related material or installing V-chips to maintain a normalized ratings system, it makes more political sense to wage a concerted effort to get girls and women on-line and educated in the technology of cyberspace in equal number with boys and men (this would be a techno-repulsion of technoppression). It is also necessary to foster resistance to sexualization (the dynamic of the deployment of sexuality) by deploying the interpretative techniques of desexualization (Marxism, feminism, and deconstruction) to confront masculinist constructions.[31] The readings that follow illustrate this latter process.

"The issue isn't whether you're paranoid. . . . The issue is whether you're paranoid enough."
—*Max Peltier*

Strange Days underscores the intersection of the deployments of alliance, sexuality, and programmed perfection and the latter's trajectory toward technoppression through a snuff clip that serves as a catalyst to its internecine plot and production of paranoia. Here SQUID, the futuristic surveillance device from technoppression, records the experience of several pathologies from within the deployment of sexuality—namely exhibitionism, voyeurism, and paranoia—through (what is filmically cast as) an actual rape and murder, a function of the system of alliance. What ensues is a mystery/horror story pivoting on questions of the killer's identity and why he is pursuing Lenny. Presented anonymously to Lenny, the clip records the killer's experience as he stalks a woman named Iris (Brigitte Baho), a sex worker who has been a recorder in a number of Lenny's clips. We, as members of the movie audience, visually join Lenny in experiencing the killer's experience and then gain distance from it as we witness his reaction to that experience. Thus "we/they" handcuff and blindfold Iris and then wire her so that she experiences the killer's highly aroused sensations as "we/they" rape and then strangle her to death.

Although this particular scene enacts certain pornographic thrill-kill elements, its critical stance also undercuts them. (This might be one of the reasons that the film was not a box office hit. By contrast, it is popular on video, which allows viewers to pause or speed up as they wish.) Its contrast to the film's various soft-core depictions are stark. Moreover, two crucial filmic moments distinguish it from formulaic rape/murder pornography. First of all, the visual participation of the audience culminates with a jarring moment when the killer reopens Iris's eyes; as the camera zooms in on her retina, we see the killer's masked head reflected where we, as viewer/participants, would otherwise be. This is an effectively disconcerting commentary on filmic identification. Secondly, from Lenny Nero's response throughout the time that he is wired up, it is clear that he is repulsed and horrified. When it is over, he bolts from the car and vomits. Given the logic of SQUID technology, the killer's thrill is also felt, but the film emphasizes Lenny's moral revulsion overcoming his orgasmic responses.

One question these scenes pose for cultural theory is whether such depictions denaturalize rape and denormalize masculinist pleasure in viewing sexual violence. I pose it this way because such claims are sometimes made about popular culture representations of cyborgs in science fiction films and cyberpunk fiction, regardless of their misogynistic features. To my mind, it is necessary to be more qualified about what constitutes resistance and more discriminating about claims of intervention. The effects of our own analytic procedure need to be taken into account. For example, in writing this essay I had to replay the scenes of sexual violence numerous times, sometimes pausing to dissect a particular point, much like the jury at the first Rodney King trial. The point made then—and that I would confirm for myself—is that such repeated viewing does diminish the shock and repulsion one feels upon witnessing violence, whether real, represented, or simulated.

While this does not necessarily mean that I or other viewers would become callous to or desire actual violence, as some anti-porn critics insist, it does not mean that the film constitutes resistance either. It does indicate that cultural analysts need to make a concerted effort to differentiate between our own desensitization from image repetition and what we label political resistance and subversion. Although I do think the rape/murder scene in *Strange Days* is directed so as to curb audience participation in the killer's sadism and enhance sympathy with his victim, its depiction oscillates between deconstructing and reinstituting masculinist brutality. This reinstatement is underscored by the end of the film which heralds the morality of the law when the police commissioner comes to the rescue. That reassurance, however, did not diminish the overall effect on me as a female viewer of an intensification of fear of sexual assault.

This kind of shuffle between deconstruction and reinscription is one of technoppression's means for concealing its power relations even as it fosters fear and paranoia. Learning how to analyze the generic conventions of horror stories and romance, however, both of which are paradigmatically apocalyptic in their movement from the production of fear to the reassurance of a new order, can help counter the effects. Typically in horror stories, a male protagonist is rendered temporarily vulnerable and unable to deter violence against a woman: he is made to watch in horror as she is brutalized. Often his greatest consternation surrounds the fate of his beloved who is under threat, the first woman then serving as a surrogate for the "more important" one. Just as typically, by the end of a horror story his manhood is restored and she is saved.[32] *Strange Days* employs these conventions and then gives them a twist. Faith has joined forces with Lenny's best friend Max Peltier (Tom Sizemore), who, it turns out, is not just a betrayer of friendship but the film's pathological killer. Thus Lenny's manhood can never be fully restored by the conventions of horror. He does manage to kill Max and defeat a force of evil. But the final fantasy of restoration remains thwarted because Faith is deemed unredeemable. As I will indicate more fully later, the conclusion of the film turns from horror to romance and thereby supplants a restoration of manhood with a sentimental feminist redefinition of manhood.

Lenny's defeat of Max represents a defeat of the brutal masculinity permitted under the system of alliance and a stopgap measure in the dominating tactics of technoppression. Sounding like a streetwise version of Baudrillard, Max is the film's mouthpiece for the prime trait of technoppression: terminal cynicism (forgive the pun). Early in the film in a bar when he toasts "To the end of all things," he remarks "I know it's the end of the world . . . cause everything's already been done." Max's downfall is that he can't resist the forces of technoppression and hence becomes their embodiment. This is most evident in his fatal fight with Lenny when his long hair is suddenly ripped off, revealing a full-time SQUID wig; no moment in his life goes unrecorded. The desire to be able to relive and foist on others his sadism is a technoppressive spin on confession, a compulsion to have an audience not just as a witness but as a co-experiencer of his acts of murderous pleasure.

Max's death brings about a temporary overturning of the truth of paranoia, a way of seeing the world that was formalized as a symptom in the therapeutic logic of the deployment of sexuality, but which is technoppression's quintessential weapon against efforts for social justice.[33] He has been the priest of paranoia, spreading the word of conspiracy in his claims about a L.A.P.D. death squad. Yet *Strange Days*'s treatment of paranoia is ultimately disingenuous. It is worth noting, however, because it is so typical. Rather than conceding that paranoia is an understandable by-product of global information banks and visual technologies capable of recording every aspect of life, from the most mundane to the pernicious or heroic, the film portrays paranoia as Max's one-man conspiracy against Lenny. Struggles against technoppression will require a stance capable of discerning the generation of paranoia as a structural element of a highly technologized society. From a genealogical perspective, activist-minded skepticism is one way to avoid a naive rush to judgment about whatever conspiracy is at hand. And skeptical activism is a way to curb the cynical defense of apathy.

Significantly, in its portrayal of male friendship and its discontents, the film once more oscillates between deconstruction and reinscription of heteronormative masculinity. Max's desire to have Lenny jack in to his acts of rape and murder of Iris and his sadomasochistic sex with Faith fuel homophobic fears and hence refortify the "safe" and "healthy" heterosexuality represented by Lenny. One way to redirect this move critically is to use it to expose the paranoia of compulsory heterosexuality, a structural element of the deployment of sexuality exemplified by the heterosexist panic over gay men in the military, where the rhetoric about same-sex showers serves as a site for simultaneous titillation and purgation.

"GOOD YEAR 2000"
— *Good Year Blimp*

What other forms of individual and collective resistance are available against technoppression? *Strange Days* suggests that a retelling of history is one, a way of recasting the past in order to reimagine the future. There is merit to this idea, but in the case of *Strange Days*, certain problems arise that warrant careful scrutiny. The most controversial element of the film is its rewriting/reimaging of the Rodney King beating. In a maneuver that burdens the film's value for political critique—although it does, albeit implausibly, underscore links between political and personal choices—this restaging unfolds through a love-conquers-all story. Unbeknownst to Lenny, though clear to the audience, Mace is in love with him.

Again, all of this revolves around a SQUID clip. As with the police assault on Rodney King, a recording device becomes a critical counter-memory tool against hegemonic claims. Through a complicated turn of events, Jeriko's manager Philo Gant, who by all accounts has become an addicted wirehead and paranoid control freak, hires Iris, who is white, to set Jeriko up as a way of regaining an upper hand over him. As it turns out, Jeriko One's growing influence and apocalyptic activism have also infuriated certain members of the L.A. police force. In this case, Iris's SQUID records two white policemen illegally stopping, harassing, and finally murdering Jeriko One as well as the other rap star and the other white woman. As the one who was given possession of the clip, which needless to say endangers his life, Lenny is forced to make a political and ethical decision about how to use it. Fortunately for him and all of Los Angeles, Lenny does not have to rely solely on his own slippery-slope ability to make just judgments.

Throughout the film, Mace functions as a well of moral fortitude and physical adroitness against the threat of impending disaster. She is depicted as a postmodern wonderwoman: trained in martial arts and an expert sharpshooter, she also has a mother's heart, a lover's sense of protectiveness, and a black-activist social conscience. Lenny is indeed in good hands. In several crucial instances, Mace comes to his rescue as if Lenny were a damsel in distress. Lenny's feminization and Mace's masculinization are retained even at the end of the film, but both are also qualified substantially, for a better normative heterosexual fit. In Lenny's case, masculine prowess returns just long enough to see him through his battle against Max. But his real transformation has already begun; it is revealed when he turns the crucial clip over to Mace rather than using it in exchange for Faith. With that action, he surrenders his personal desire for the sake of social justice, an ethical decision he has become capable of because of Mace's influence. She too undergoes a shift in moral ground when she agrees to experience Iris's SQUID clip. Up to that point, she has categorically condemned the use of SQUID technology. Her shift signifies an important counterhegemonic reminder that technology can be a vital tool against technoppression.

Unfortunately, the importance of Mace's decision gets buried as the drama is given over to Lenny's struggle. The conventions of horror are at this point reoriented toward an apocalyptic motif of male spiritual victory in which the man must turn away from the fallen woman. Only then can he be rewarded with the good woman. The ur-narrative for this age-old plot is depicted in the Book of Revelation with the defeat of the Whore of Babylon, who is, not so unlike Faith, "arrayed in purple and scarlet colour, and decked with gold and precious stones and pearls, having a golden cup in her hand full of abominations and filthiness of her fornication" (17:4). The clearly electist reward there is to allow the 144,000 men who have maintained their purity to enter into the New

Jerusalem, which is to be "prepared as a bride adorned for her husband" (21:2). Although notably sexier in a glittering black, mini-skirted cocktail dress, but no less pure of heart and soul, Mace does finally receive Lenny in an embrace that marks the arrival of the new millennium.

But not before defeating the forces of evil and rerighting, by rewriting, history. In the most implausible move of the film, and following Lenny's assurance that the L.A.P.D. Commissioner Palmer Strickland is, as his name suggests, a strict upholder of the law of the stricken land, Mace entrusts the clip and a SQUID cap to the commissioner. But she is forced to flee before knowing what he will do with it. A chase scene leads her finally, just minutes before the turn of the millennium, to a final confrontation with the two killer cops. Putting up a remarkable fight in which she actually manages to handcuff them to a steel guardrail, she is nonetheless eventually cornered by a squadron of police, fully armed for attack. Then comes the restaged Rodney King scene, so implanted by repetition in our minds and up to this point given confirmation by the killing of Jeriko One. But this time it is Mace who is beaten to the ground, kicked to stay down, and hit with batons. And this time, a rebellion breaks out on the spot, inaugurated by a black child who refuses to allow the injustice. And, finally and most apocalyptically, this time, just as all hell breaks loose, peace is restored by the appearance of Commissioner Strickland. Holding the clip up as if it were his badge, he saves the day.

And Mace gets her man. But as I said earlier, Lenny is now a "new man." No longer a self-pitying and exploitive corrupter of values, his retention of a touch of femininity, symbolized by his fainting after he has valiantly shielded her body against gunshot with his own, is also an assurance that he will not try to overtake her with male authority. His epiphany of love for Mace arrives with the millennium. The film ends with their passionate kiss as the Good Year blimp floats across the night sky, a backdrop for the announcement that the 'New Era' has begun.

"A New day is coming."
—Jeriko One

Is this ending defensible or just plain hokey? I suppose it could be defended aesthetically as a parodic postmodern fairy tale or an intertextual allusion to *Blade-Runner* and other films. But such accountings can only go so far. I admit to finding the final scene emotionally satisfying as a romance and a relief after all that suspense and slaughter—yet facile too. Perhaps those judgments are, finally, beside the point or too targeted to the domain of film appreciation; they lead to a simplistic thumbs-up or thumbs-down response. After all, even though it has an apocalyptically romantic ending, *Strange Days* does bring up some of the most vexing issues of our time. So, as a way of concluding this discussion, I want to indicate how the ending of *Strange Days* prompts consideration of a technique integral to programmed perfection: morphing. What happens when morphing is deployed by technoppressive forces in order to dominate?

Reading the film's final scenes from a genealogical skeptical perspective highlights an important way that technoppression conceals one means of domination and expansion: by morphing history. History gets morphed, for example, in the film's retelling/reimaging of the Rodney King video, trials, and rebellion. There are of course, more explicit cinematic examples of this process in which digital effects falsify history; *Zelig* and *Forrest Gump* are two that come to mind, each of which self-reflexively expose the process at work (which is not the same as an ideological expose). A number of Oliver Stone's films also morph history, creating a whole new representation that replaces the sources from which it derives. Needless to say, movies are hardly alone in this process of historical erasure.

Technoppression also uses morphing as a way of mythologizing the state of health of the cultural body politic. For example, Commissioner Strickland's "cavalry-to-the-rescue" arrival promotes faith in the good white father as proper guardian of public welfare. Despite the theme of deep corruption within the police force that the film develops, the depiction of goodness at the top undermines the activist portrayals represented by Jeriko One and Mace. When Mace turns to Strickland as her champion, activism is replaced by a reassertion of authority of the white-controlled state. Jeriko One's populist form of activism is at that point reenvisioned as a threat.

Technoppression also uses morphing on behalf of genetic control, again in the name of perfection. A eugenic principle is at work in its prediction of the future appearance of a multicultural United States, with a completely racially mixed (and hence "raceless") citizenry. In technoppression's form of genetic prophecy, racial conflict is portrayed as the by-product of biological determinism rather than unequal social relations; on this view, a change in biology is all that is needed.[34] Something of this view is suggested in the interracial fairy-tale ending of *Strange Days*. Lenny and Mace's symbolic status as the new Adam and Eve for the twenty-first century pitches the film from its dystopian vision of race war in the last days of the twentieth century onto a utopian horizon for the new millennium.

Even though such morphings pose significant threats to democratic decision making, it is worth repeating that the power techniques within technoppression give rise to possibilities of resistance to it. In other words, it is not the technique of morphing that threatens freedom. Whether it is for purposes of bodily surgery or even reimagining history, morphing is merely a technological way to imagine something new coming into existence. Problems arise when the technique reinforces or newly constitutes oppressive power/knowledge relations by monumentalizing history, mythologizing the cultural body politic, or negating bodily differences in the name of homogeneous perfection.

Like any narrative or imagistic revisioning, morphing has the potential to empower as well as disenfranchise. Perhaps, then, it is possible to morph the final kiss at the end of *Strange Days* for nonapocalyptic purposes. It is, after all, right up there with the great screen kisses of all times. What would it take to make the utopian image of their kiss crossfade into an image of commitment to democratic freedom? At a minimum, such politically attuned morphing calls for a critical practice of struggles against all three of the power deployments of alliance, sexuality, and programmed perfection. The countertruth of skeptical morphing may lack the instant fix of technoppression's deception, but it has the merit of knowing that every day is a new day, a strange day, a day of reckoning.

EPILOGUE
SKEPTICISM AS A WAY OF LIFE

To celebrate having lived half a century, I decided to give sky-diving a try. To be on the safe side, I determined that a tandem jump made the most sense, and, to help bolster my courage, asked my friend Marie-France Etienne if she would join the adventure. As it turned out, it was something she had always wanted to do. The experience proved more exhilarating than anything I had even wildly imagined, with my senses heightened to a point of delicious terror and my mind so riveted to the instant that even a year later I can recall the most minute details of the air against my face and the exquisite color variations in the lakes and land below.

Now, I wouldn't say that hurling oneself to the ground from 10,000 feet in the air is in any way *necessary* to the practice of skepticism. But, since I was in the thick of thinking through this book, I did place my experience in that context. In that light, I found one particular moment of my sky dive especially revealing. It was, quite literally, a threshold moment, a blink-of-the-eye flash of revelation that occurred in between huddling at the open door of the plane and leaping out into the cold, sun-lit air. That fraction of a second was an intense encounter with the "I don't know." In this case, "I don't know" encapsulated several possibilities all at once: "I don't know if I can do this"; "I don't know if I should do this"; and "I don't know if I will live through it." For an advocate of skepticism, of course, "I don't know" is hardly an admission of defeat. Rather, it is one of the pillars of skeptical thought, a reminder that we live with uncertainty about lots of things, especially the most meaningful things, like the time of our own death or whether someone we love, loves us.

I have wanted to draw on that sense of "I don't know" throughout this book. As a method of inquiry, skepticism's insistence that we always live in the "I don't know" exposes the leading ways in which apocalyptic and millennialist belief shape everyday life to the detriment of democratic freedom. For the kind of skepticism I have been advocating, recognizing that we live in the "I don't know" can serve as a useful tool for putting into doubt what others claim to know without any doubt, from the proper way to have sex, to what the future holds, to when the world will end. Acknowledging that we live in the "I don't know" is a direct challenge to the claims of certainty inherent in apocalyptic knowledge. Living in the "I don't know" of skepticism questions organizations of knowledge that are built on the edifice of apocalypse.

Genealogically-minded skepticism confronts with doubt the most profound promise of apocalyptic revelation, the moment of Truth unveiled, the blinding flash toward which all history has been leading. The apocalyptic unveiling is a covenant with catastrophe, yet it has been made alluring through its pledge to the true believers that this world-shattering moment is not only necessary but worth it. This vision has a canny mode of persuasion: With the cataclysm comes the great and final revelation of Truth, reserved for the elect alone, the new and perfect era, the Millennium. In contrast, the doubt integral to skepticism fortifies itself by gathering historical evidence, attending to the ways that contradictions and inconsistencies leak out of the narrative containers of universal Truth. Skeptical truth, in other words, is possible, but contingent, necessary and yet constantly in need of reevaluation and change to meet changing times. Against apocalyptic hubris, skepticism may strike some as too humble. But this very humility becomes compelling when one recognizes apocalyptic and millennialist belief as an affront to open inquiry and a roadblock to democracy.

As crucial as living in the "I don't know" is to skepticism, skepticism *as a way of life* requires more from us. By highlighting the ways that skeptical thought shapes the meanings of life events, I have also argued that skeptical thought bestows the blessing that Prior Walter gives at the conclusion of *Angels in America*: "More Life." I want to return to my skydiving adventure to help illustrate what I mean. This time what interests me is not the dive itself, but two experiences surrounding the dive, because they literally brought home, that is, brought into my home, how skepticism fosters a more meaningful life.

I have to back up a bit to tell this part of the story, to indicate what happened when I announced my skydiving plans to my sons. They were, at best, apprehensive about it. Since they are reasonable men, then in their late twenties, I value their opinions, but I was nevertheless determined to fulfill what really was a life-long dream. Given my sons' reactions, I decided not to worry my parents in advance. My oldest son, however, concluded that since his appeals had not worked to change my mind, perhaps my parents could do the trick. My mother and father had no hesitation about weighing in vehemently against what they regarded as far too dangerous and damned foolhardy. Their late-night phone call before my scheduled morning jump was agonizing. As it turned out, inclement weather postponed it anyway. In the interim, my anxious mother began to send me news clippings on recent injuries and fatalities associated with the sport. Although skydiving is relatively safe, she was able to find a pretty steady assortment of mishaps. So when I rescheduled my new appointment in the spring, I simply decided not to tell any of them this time around. But then I was stuck with the possibility that I would join the ranks of the dead without having said a word about it to them!

That's when I decided to leave a death note. It wasn't a will or even an organ donation statement, which I already had, it was one of those "if you are reading this, there are some things I want to say" kinds of notes. Most of what I wrote, I am pretty sure they already believed, like how deeply I love them, but I also wanted them to grasp that, even though I didn't think I was going to die, since the statistics were well on the side of safety, if I did, I had no regret about having, albeit inadvertently, orchestrated the moment. Indeed, I felt that this might be what is sometimes called a "good death." And from reflecting on my life in this way, I felt its richness more keenly then ever. So I wrote my note and placed it on my dining room table so that my younger son, who lives nearby, would eventually find it. Since I lived through my jump, of course, I was the one to find it, right there where I put it.

It is an odd feeling to read your own "final thoughts." Being able to do so means they are superfluous, but in my case they seemed especially so. It was not as though I had attained the kind of wisdom that can accrue from living through a horrible illness or gained the sort of ethical confidence that sometimes derives from saving oneself or someone else from danger. What I did have, in addition to a jolly good time, was the salutary effect of seeing what might have been my final thoughts rendered not only not final but, in a sense, not meaningful. My sentiments remained heartfelt. But the context had changed. Reading them after my jump was a little embarrassing. I chucked the note into the recycling bin, and went on with everyday things.

Nevertheless, the experience remained with me, like an annoying itch or bit of dust in my eye, and cropped up again as I began writing this epilogue. I have learned to cue into such intellectual irritants, so I asked myself, how might writing that note be understood in light of skepticism? Posing the question that way led me to see another element vital to skepticism: living in the "just in case." For some people, living in the "just in case" has metaphysical application on the order of "just in case God exists and there is a hell, I won't deny his existence and will live according to divine mandates." That isn't what I mean. Living with "just in case" as a skeptical attitude toward life and death highlights our agency and its links to others. At its most dramatic, it is a "just in case I die, I want to have done this, or said the following." The rationale is not to follow divine morality but, rather, to forge human ethics. I wrote my death note to help console people I care deeply about in the remote event that my jump proved fatal. Writing the note forced me to grapple with a conflict between my choice and my family's wishes. There was no clear, single answer but, rather, several possible ways to deal with the conflict. I chose one. But I also left a "just in case" message.

In retrospect, I have come to regard "just in case" as a commendable standard of judgment in making decisions about all sorts of things on a personal and societal level. In the way that living in the "I don't know" is skepticism's epistemological foundation, living in the "just in case" is skepticism's ethical position. "Just in case" describes the kind of agency available to skepticism as a way of life. It is a skeptic's rationale for acting in a world in which "I don't know" is the primary condition. I think this holds regardless of whether one is embroiled in far more life-threatening circumstances than a skydive—or far less. By making decisions and acting on the basis of "I don't know" but "just in case" we acknowledge these profound truths: some commitments are worth making both to ourselves and to others, they often conflict, and there are no guarantees. Much if not most of the time, we live without reflecting on any of this, even putting forward a faith in the opposite, acting as if we know outcomes and being apathetic about commitments that we otherwise hold dear. But skepticism as a way of life both asks for and gives something more. Together, the two stances of "I don't know" and "just in case" provide the grounds for skeptical activism. Under these circumstances, there is no single cause, but many commitments, some overlapping, some competing.

Skepticism understood this way makes democracy possible as an everyday practice. As such, skepticism offers its own compelling promises of personal and social satisfaction. Acting on the basis of uncertainty can be more exhilarating than enacting the dogma of apocalypse if we come to appreciate liberty and equality over the regime of the elect. Realizing that the dream of the Great Millennium not only defers but blocks democratic process can serve as an enticement to a different dream, a dream of commitment to the practice of freedom. There can be great reassurance in knowing that technology is neither beast nor savior but what we make of it. Breathless excitement can accompany the recognition that our sense of self is traceable to historical and cultural forces, and that if we change those conditions of everyday life, we change ourselves. It can be stirring to understand that when we make such changes on a larger scale, in public education, economic reform, and political governance, we transform society. As a check on naive optimism on the one hand and needless pessimism on the other, skepticism as a way of life may just be the most exciting prospect the third millennium has to offer.

Notes

Introduction: Threshold of Revelation

1. Ted Daniels, "Selling Capital's Apocalypse: Y2K Tool," *Millennial Prophecy Report* 6, no. 4 (January 1998):67.
2. *Time* magazine is a useful register of these trends. See, for example, its coverage of El Niño in the February 16, 1998, issue and cover stories, such as "Does Heaven Exist?" (March 24, 1997) and "Jesus Online" (December 16, 1996).
3. For an excellent discussion of endism in Fundamentalist Christian and New Age belief, see Charles Strozier, *Apocalypse: On the Psychology of Fundamentalism in America* (Boston: Beacon, 1994).
4. In some instances of New Age thought, there is a catastrophic end, in keeping with apocalyptic disaster, either divinely, naturally, or technologically brought about. In these scenarios, the elect are usually those said to have attained transcendence.
5. Stephen Jay Gould in an interview with Robert Kulrich at the 92nd Street YMCA, September 21, 1997, telecast on C-span, January 1, 1998. See Gould's *Questioning the Millennium* (Note 6).
6. Gould's book is informative and charmingly written, but it also lacks discussion about the ways that apocalyptic belief functions within cultures to cast certain groups as the enemy through what I am calling electism. See Stephen Jay Gould, *Questioning the Millennium: A Rationalist Guide to a Precisely Arbitrary Countdown* (New York: Harmony Books, 1997).
7. This is not to ignore the ways in which both religious and secular apocalypse have also been used by women and minorities to foster liberation, as

I indicated in *Anti-Apocalypse* and as other scholars have argued; see in particular, Catherine Keller, *Apocalypse Now and Then: A Feminist Guide to the End of the World* (Boston: Beacon Press, 1996); and James Berger, *After the End: Representations of Post-Apocalypse* (Minneapolis: University of Minnesota Press, 1999). It is to insist, however, in some contrast to both Keller and Berger, that apocalypticism is structured around an electism that thwarts equality by pitting the elected group against its enemy (or anyone within its own camp who aligns with the enemy). This is one reason why, historically, when liberatory gains have occurred through apocalyptic inspiration, they have soon suffered fragmentation or dogmatic centralization. Furthermore, apocalyptic truth has far more widely produced and justified patriarchal, racist, and homosexual oppression than it has countered them.

8. Norman Cohn, *The Pursuit of the Millennium* (New York: Oxford University Press, 1970). See the Conclusion in particular, which was added to this revised edition.

9. Gould discusses several instances of marginalized groups that have been moved by the powerful promise of the Christian apocalypse toward armed struggle, only to be massacred. See *Questioning the Millennium*, pp. 52–62.

10. John Rajchman, *Michel Foucault: The Freedom of Philosophy* (New York: Columbia University Press, 1985), p. 4.

1. Skeptical Revelations of an American Feminist on Patmos

1. Lee Quinby, *Anti-Apocalypse: Exercises in Genealogical Criticism* (Minneapolis: University of Minnesota Press, 1994).

2. Ernest Tuveson, *Redeemer Nation: The Idea of America's Millennial Role* (Chicago: University of Chicago Press, 1966); Sacvan Bercovitch, *The American Jeremiad* (Madison: University of Wisconsin Press, 1975).

3. Nathan O. Hatch, "The Origins of Civil Millennialism in America: New England Clergymen, War with France, and the Revolution," *William and Mary Quarterly* 31 (1974): 407–30.

4. Stephen D. O'Leary, *Arguing the Apocalypse: A Theory of Millennial Rhetoric* (New York: Oxford University Press, 1994); Paul Boyer, *When Time Shall Be No More: Prophecy Belief in Contemporary American Culture* (Cambridge: Harvard University Press, 1992); also see Charles Strozier, *Apocalypse: On the Psychology of Fundamentalism in America* (Boston: Beacon Press, 1994).

5. For an excellent overview of cultural trends surrounding the year 2000, see Kevin McClure, *The Fortean Times Book of the Millennium* (London: John Brown Publishing, 1996).

6. The debate about whether January 1, 2000, or January 1, 2001, is the beginning of the new millennium stems from the adoption of the Gregorian calendar, which had no designation for a year 0 between 1 B.C. and 1 A.D.

7. See Gwendolyn K. Shamblin, "Weight Loss through Spiritual Gain" and Paula Downey Suddeath, "How I Broke the Food Chain," in *Christian Woman*, May/June 1995, pp. 80–83. Thanks to Jodi Dean for obtaining this material for me.

8. For an excellent treatment of the effects of the year 1000 on European culture, see Richard Landes, *Relics, Apocalypse, and the Deceits of History* (Cambridge: Harvard University Press, 1995); and for a fascinating sweep of end-of-century responses over the last millennium, see Hillel Schwartz, *Century's End* (New York: Doubleday, 1996).

9. On ufology and alien abduction, see Jodi Dean, *Aliens in America* (Ithaca: Cornell University Press, 1998); for the largest archive of sightings and millennial information in the 1990s, see Ted Daniels, ed., *Millennial Prophecy Report* [http://www.channel1.com/mpr].

10. Norman Cohn, *Cosmos, Chaos, and the World to Come: The Ancient Roots of Apocalyptic Faith* (New Haven: Yale University Press, 1993), chap. 12.

11. Archimandrite Theodoritos Bournis, "I was in the isle of Patmos . . . " (Athens: Alex. Matsoukis S.A., 1992), p. 35.

2. Teaching on the Threshold: *Angels* and Skeptics

1. Adam Phillips, "Besides Good and Evil," in *On Flirtation* (Cambridge: Harvard University Press, 1994), p. 64.

2. Tony Kushner, *Angels in America: Part One: Millennium Approaches* (New York: Theatre Communications Group), p. 33.

3. I want to thank the students who have taken this class and been so important to my thinking about this issue. I also thank Mary Katherine Wainwright for her suggestions on an earlier draft.

4. David Savran, "Ambivalence, Utopia, and a Queer Sort of Materialism: How *Angels in America* Reconstructs the Nation," *Theatre Journal* 47 (1995): 219.

5. Tony Kushner, *Angels in America: Part Two: Perestroika* (New York: Theatre Communications Group, 1994), p. 146.

6. Ibid. p. 145.

7. Norman Cohn, *Cosmos, Chaos, and the World to Come: The Ancient Roots of Apocalyptic Faith* (New Haven: Yale University Press, 1993); Paul Boyer, *When Time Shall Be No More: Prophecy Belief in Modern American Culture* (Cambridge: Harvard University Press, 1992); Tina Pippin, *Death and Desire: The Rhetoric of Gender in the Apocalypse of John* (Louisville: John Knox

Press, 1992); Hal Lindsey, *The Late Great Planet Earth* (Grand Rapids, Mich.: Zondervan, 1970); and Charles Strozier, *Apocalypse: On the Psychology of Fundamentalism in America* (Boston: Beacon Press, 1994).

8. For an insightful exploration of Kushner's calling into "question Jewish male morality in the postmodern era" (30), see Jyl Lynn Felman, "Lost Jewish (Male) Souls, *Tikkun* 10 (May/June 1995): 27–30.

9. Tony Kushner, interview by Andrea Bernstein, *Mother Jones* (July/August 1995), p. 64.

10. Kushner, *Perestroika*, p. 61.

11. Margaret Urban Walker, *Moral Understandings: A Feminist Study in Ethics* (New York: Routledge, 1998), p. 223.

12. Kushner, *Perestroika*, p. 67.

13. Toni Morrison, *Playing in the Dark* (Cambridge: Harvard University Press, 1990), p. ix.

3. Genealogical Skepticism: How Theory Confronts Millennialism

1. Tony Kushner, *Angels in America: Part Two: Perestroika* (New York: Theatre Communications Group, 1992): pp. 13–14.

2. Gertrude Stein, *Ida* (New York: Vintage, 1941), p. 132.

3. Ben Yagoda, "Retooling Critical Theory: Buddy, Can You Paradigm?" *New York Times*, 4 September 1994, section K, p. 6.

4. Ibid.

5. On A.L.S.C., see Richard Lacayo, "War of Words," *Time*, 7 July 1997, p. 92, and on both groups see, Denise Magner, "Ten Years of Defending the Classics and Fighting Political Correctness," *Chronicle of Higher Education*, 12 December 1997, pp. A12–14.

6. In "Theory as Liberatory Practice," bell hooks makes an argument of this sort by charging that "it is indeed the purpose of such theory [the most highly visible feminist theory] to divide, separate, exclude, keep at a distance." In *Teaching to Transgress: Education as the Practice of Freedom* (New York: Routledge, 1994), p. 65.

7. Gerald Graff, "Why Theory?" in *Left Politics and the Literary Profession*, ed. Lennard Davis and M. Bella Mirabella (New York: Columbia University Press, 1990), pp. 20–35.

8. For an astute refutation of this view of theory, see John McGowan, *Postmodernism and Its Critics* (Ithaca: Cornell University Press, 1991), p. 205.

9. From another perspective, Martha Nussbaum makes a case for the importance of metaphysics, "which we might loosely describe as the activity of analyzing the most general concepts that we use in talking and thinking about

anything whatever, concepts such as cause and effect, substance and property, and so forth." Her criticism that some feminists have grown too suspicious of general concepts seems apt to me, but her espousal of metaphysics lacks a sufficient calculation of power/knowledge forces in the production of these concepts. This is not surprising, given her anti-Foucauldian stance in this article. See Nussbaum, "Feminists and Philosophy," *New York Review of Books*, 20 October 1994, p. 62.

10. Michel Foucault, "Two Lectures," in *Power/Knowledge: Selected Interviews and Other Writings, 1972–1977*, ed. Colin Gordon (New York: Pantheon, 1980), p. 83. Foucault's most sustained discussion is in "Nietzsche, Genealogy, History," in *Language, Counter-Memory, Practice*, ed. Donald F. Bouchard (Ithaca: Cornell University Press, 1977), pp. 138–64.

11. Nancy K. Miller, "Autobiography as Cultural Criticism," in *Getting Personal: Feminist Occasions and Other Autobiographical Acts* (New York: Routledge, 1991), pp. 1–30.

12. David Mason, "Mythical Histories," *Hudson Review* (Winter 1993): 660–61.

13. In this sense *Jazz* performs the task of genealogy that Foucault calls "analysis of descent," by studying the "numberless beginnings whose faint traces and hints of color are readily seen by an historical eye. The analysis of descent permits the dissociation of the self, its recognition and displacement as an empty synthesis, in liberating a profusion of lost events." Foucault, "Nietzsche, Genealogy, History," pp. 145–46.

14. Toni Morrison, *Jazz* (New York: Alfred Knopf, 1992), pp. 139–40.

15. Morrison, *Jazz*, p. 228.

16. Evan Simpson and Mark Williams, "The Ideal of Social Disillusionment," *Philosophical Forum* 26, no. 1 (Fall 1994): 74–75.

17. See "Interview with Lucette Finas," in *Michel Foucault, Power, Truth, Strategy*, ed. Meaghan Morris and Paul Patton, trans. Paul Foss and Meaghan Morris (Sydney: Feral Publications, 1979), pp. 74–75.

18. Garry Wills, *Inventing America: Jefferson's Declaration of Independence* (New York: Doubleday, 1978).

4. Millennialist Morality and the Problem of Chastity

1. *Donahue*, 27 January 1994.

2. Judith Newman, "Proud to Be a Virgin," *New York Times*, 19 June 1994, Styles section, p. 1.

3. Harmful appropriations of multiculturalism by conservative forces show up clearly enough when we consider that, in the name of multiculturalism, funding often goes toward corporatism in public schools rather than pro-

grams to eliminate race and gender bias in school curricula or plans to equitably distribute tax dollars. Henry A. Giroux has dealt extensively with such right-wing appropriations. See, for example, his *Fugitive Cultures: Race, Violence, and Youth* (New York: Routledge, 1996).

4. Public Law 104–193, Section 519 of Title V of the U.S. Social Security Act (as amended on August 22, 1996). President Clinton increased financial support in January 1997 through advocacy of a "National Strategy to Prevent Teen Pregnancy" that promotes "abstinence until marriage." See the *SIECUS REPORT* (August/September 1997) for further information from the perspective of proponents for comprehensive sexuality education.

5. Clare Saliba, "How the Welfare Bill Could Change the Way Teenagers Learn about Sex," *Village Voice*, 21 January 1997.

6. For an excellent example of the kind of history I am espousing, see Lori D. Ginzberg, "'The Hearts of Your Readers Will Shudder': Fanny Wright, Infidelity, and American Freethought," *American Quarterly* 46 (June 1994): 195–226.

7. Michel Foucault, *The Use of Pleasure, The History of Sexuality, Volume Two,* trans. Robert Hurley (New York: Pantheon, 1985), p. 30. For an extended discussion of Thoreau's aesthetics of chastity, see "The Care of the Chaste Self: Thoreau's *Walden* and the Desexualization of Masculinity," in Lee Quinby, *Freedom, Foucault, and the Subject of America* (Boston: Northeastern University Press, 1991).

8. Stephen Nissenbaum, *Sex, Diet, and Debility in Jacksonian America: Sylvester Graham and Health Reform* (Westport, Conn.: Greenwood Press, 1980).

9. For a concise review of this movement, see John D'Emilio and Estelle B. Freedman, *Intimate Matters: A History of Sexuality in America* (New York: Harper & Row, 1988), chap. 9.

10. "Judgment Call," quoted in "The Chastity Revolution," *Reader's Digest* 140 (May 1992), p. 71.

11. Elizabeth Larsen, "Censoring Sex Information: The Story of *Sassy*," *Utne Reader*, July/August 1990, pp. 96–97.

12. Marc Cooper, "Chastity 101," *Village Voice*, 7 June 1994, pp. 1, 31–35; Philip Elmer-Dewitt, "Making the Case for Abstinence," *Time*, 24 May 1994, pp. 64–65.

13. Cooper, "Chastity 101," p. 32; and the *SIECUS REPORT.*

14. For an extended discussion of how Christian fundamentalism incorporates misogyny, racism, and homophobia, see Lee Quinby, *Anti-Apocalypse: Exercises in Genealogical Criticism* (Minneapolis: University of Minnesota Press, 1994).

15. Cooper, "Chastity 101," p. 31.

16. Elmer-Dewitt, "Making the Case for Abstinence," p. 65.

17. Sylvester Graham, *A Lecture to Young Men, on Chastity, intended also for the serious consideration of parents and guardians* (Providence, 1834), pp. 78–79; and quoted in Nissenbaum, pp. 106–7.

18. Newman, "Proud to Be a Virgin."

19. Julia Phillips, "You'll Never Get Laid in This Town Again: Why No One's Having Sex in Hollywood," *Gentlemen's Quarterly*, March 1991, pp. 146–47.

20. Mary Patricia Barth Fourqurean, "Chastity as Shared Strength: An Open Letter to Students," *America*, 6 November 1993, p. 10.

21. Veronica Chambers, "Young, Hot, and Celibate," *Essence*, July 1993, p. 56.

22. For the text of the letter to Blake, see *The Correspondence of Henry David Thoreau*, ed. Walter Harding and Carl Bode (New York: New York University Press, 1958), p. 288. For the two essays, see Henry D. Thoreau, *Early Essays and Miscellanies*, ed. Joseph J. Moldenhauer et al. (Princeton: Princeton University Press, 1975), pp. 268–75. References to "Chastity and Sensuality" hereafter cited parenthetically in the text.

23. This is the overview provided by Walter Harding and Michael Meyer, *The New Thoreau Handbook* (New York: New York University Press, 1980), p. 151.

24. Charles Anderson, "Thoreau's Monastic Vows," *Etudes Anglaises* 22 (1969): 11.

25. Richard Bridgman, *Dark Thoreau* (Lincoln: University of Nebraska Press, 1982), p. 121.

26. James Armstrong, "Thoreau, Chastity, and the Reformers," in *Thoreau's Psychology*, ed. Raymond D. Gozzi (Boston: University Press of America, 1983), p. 125.

27. Richard Lebeaux, *Thoreau's Seasons* (Amherst: University of Massachusetts Press, 1984), p. 176.

28. This is Mary Elkins Moller's view, for example. She argues that Thoreau's attitude toward women carried a profound ambivalence as well, ranging from misogyny to love to idealization. Comparing his view of sex to his view of women, she states, if "we examine his pronouncements on sex and other indications of his thinking and feeling, about sexual activity and his own sexuality, the ambivalence is equally startling." See her essay, "Thoreau, Womankind, and Sexuality," *ESQ* 22 (1976): 123.

29. Walter Harding, "Thoreau's Sexuality," *Journal of Homosexuality* 21 (1991): 40–41.

30. Ibid.

31. Ibid., pp. 44–45, n. 76

32. Michel Foucault, *The History of Sexuality*, trans. Robert Hurley (New York: Vintage Books, 1978), pp. 79, 104–5.

33. A variation on this theory may be seen in Ross J. Pudaloff's argument. Although he explicitly asserts disagreement with the Freudian model and

seeks to replace it with Foucault's concept of sexuality as a discursive event, it eventuates into pretty much the same thing in such comments as the following: "Thoreau underwent a discipline through which bodily needs and sexual desire were transformed by the Reason of the poet." See his "Thoreau's Composition of the Narrator: From Sexuality to Language," *Bucknell Review* 29 (1985): 124.

34. Jonathan Ned Katz, *Gay American History*, rev. ed. (New York: Meridian, 1992), pp. 481–94.

35. Foucault, *History of Sexuality*, p. 23.

36. *The Journal of Henry D. Thoreau*, ed. Bradford Torrey and Francis H. Allen (Boston: Houghton Mifflin, 1949), p. 185.

37. Harding and Meyer, *The New Thoreau Handbook*, p. 46.

38. Henry D. Thoreau, *Journal 2* (Princeton: Princeton University Press, 1981): 245.

39. There are numerous accounts of this relationship and possible marriage proposal in the various biographies. The homoerotic triangle, to use Eve Sedgwick's concept from *Between Men: English Literature and Male Homosocial Desire* (New York: Columbia University Press, 1985), was further complicated by Thoreau's response to Ellen Sewell's young brother, Edmund.

40. Richard Lebeaux, for example, argues that Thoreau's discussion equates sexuality with lust and "devolves into a justification for celibacy." See Lebeaux, *Thoreau's Seasons*, p. 177.

41. Robert D. Richardson, Jr., makes this point from Mary Douglas. See *Henry Thoreau: A Life of the Mind* (Berkeley: University of California Press, 1986), p. 269.

42. Frank P. Stearns, *Sketches from Concord and Appledore* (New York, 1895), p. 26, quoted in Harding, "Thoreau's Sexuality," p. 24.

43. Anderson, p. 11; and Richardson, p. 268.

44. F. O. Matthiessen, *American Renaissance* (New York: Oxford, 1941), p. 87.

45. Ibid., p. 91.

46. Lebeaux, *Thoreau's Seasons*, p. 177.

47. For a useful discussion of the "perfectionism" of the social reform movements of this period, including the Neo-Malthusians, see Linda Gordon, *Woman's Body, Woman's Right: Birth Control in America* (New York: Penguin, 1977), pp. 83–84.

48. Michel Foucault calls for this kind of search in order to explore moral experiences not based on the subject in the way that modern morality has been. He comments that the "search for styles of existence as different as possible from each other appears to me to be one of the points around which contemporary research could be initiated on particular groups in the past. The

search for a form of morality that would be acceptable to everyone—in the sense that everyone would have to submit to it—strikes me as catastrophic." "The Return to Morality," in *Foucault Live*, trans. John Johnston, ed. Sylvere Lotringer (New York: Semiotext(e), 1989), p. 330.

49. Henry D. Thoreau, *Walden* (Princeton: Princeton University Press, 1973), p. 71.

5. Coercive Purity: The Dangerous Promise of Apocalyptic Masculinity

1. David Van Biema, "Full of Promise," *Time*, 6 November 1995, pp. 62–63.
2. This is not the first time that a men-only religious movement has been organized, however. In 1911 and 1912, the Men and Religion Forward Movement had more than 1 million people attend their events which were organized to bring men into Protestant churches. Whereas they sought to combat the feminization of religion, Promise Keepers are fighting the feminist-ization of values. See Gail Bederman, "'The Women Have Had Charge of the Church Work Long Enough': The Men and Religion Forward Movement of 1911–1912 and the Masculinization of Middle-Class Protestantism," *American Quarterly* 41 (September 1989): 432–65.
3. www.promisekeepers.org/media/staffing.htm
4. Scott Raab's *GQ* piece points this out humorously but makes it clear that religious tolerance of non-Christian values is not a Promise Keepers principle. See Scott Raab, *GQ*, January 1996, 110–17, 127–30.
5. Donna Minkowitz's assessment of Promise Keepers is shortsighted in this regard. Although I agree with her argument that feminists need "to understand the contradictory impulses that have brought [Promise Keepers] swarming to the stadiums," I find her analysis of the group too forbearing. She seems torn between a positive response to the experience of love she witnessed among the men and that she herself felt while attending one of their rallies (in drag) and the male supremacist and homophobic aspects of their program. This particular paradox of love and hatred is endemic to apocalypticism, in which contradictoriness has rarely been an obstacle to oppressive power relations. Her view that the group's contradictoriness may mean that they "may have themselves caught in a quasi-feminist whirlwind" is unfoundedly optimistic. See Minkowitz, "In the Name of the Father," *Ms.*, November/December 1995, pp. 64–71.
6. Lee Quinby, *Anti-Apocalypse: Exercises in Genealogical Criticism* (Minneapolis: University of Minnesota Press, 1994).
7. Brian Peterson, "God Will Do His Part," Editor's Page, *New Man* September/October 1995, p. 8.
8. Michael Andre Bernstein approaches similar issues in *Foregone Conclusions: Against Apocalyptic History* (Los Angeles: University of California, 1994). He

employs the term *sideshadowing* much in the same way that I use *genealogy* and offers a particularly important critique of how apocalyptic history diminishes our understanding of the complexity and contingency of our lives.

9. Foucault puts this succinctly when he says, "Let us give the term *genealogy* to the union of erudite knowledge and local memories which allows us to establish a historical knowledge of struggles and to make use of this knowledge tactically today." Michel Foucault, "Two Lectures," in *Power/Knowledge*, ed. Colin Gordon (New York: Pantheon, 1980), pp. 82–83.

10. Phillip Greven, *Spare the Child: The Religious Roots of Punishment and the Psychological Impact of Physical Abuse* (New York: Alfred A. Knopf, 1991).

11. Special thanks go to Betty Bayer and Susan Henking who, by giving this to me for a birthday present, introduced me to the world of X-men.

12. TM and Toy Biz, Inc., Marvel Entertainment Group, 1995.

13. I would like to thank Kent Worcester for providing me with a brief history of the X-Men. His work demonstrates some of the links between "outsider media," popular culture, and the formation of masculinity. The term *rehabilitation of masculinity* is drawn from his presentation at NYSPSA Conference, April 15, 1995.

14. See Elayne Rapping's valuable discussion of the secular men's movement in regard to their assimilation of certain feminist values alongside their failure to reflect on the socioeconomic power relations that most affect men's lives. *The Culture of Recovery: Making Sense of the Self-Help Movement in Women's Lives* (Boston: Beacon, 1996), pp. 167–74.

15. See David F. Aberle, "A Note on Relative Deprivation Theory as Applied to Millenarian and Other Cult Movements," in *Millennial Dreams in Action: Studies in Revolutionary Religious Movements*, ed. Sylvia L. Thrupp (New York: Schocken Books, 1970), pp. 208–14.

16. Genealogy, in turn, gains insight from greater psychological awareness. It has emerged as antipsychological, in part because of Foucault's important critique of psychology as a disciplinary power, but when analysis foregoes psychological resonance altogether, it loses descriptive force for clarifying the nature of subjectivity as culturally defined.

17. For a full discussion of the shortcomings of the fundamentalist self as a totalistic view, see Robert Jay Lifton, *The Protean Self: Human Resilience in an Age of Fragmentation* (New York: Basic Books, 1993), chapter 9; and Charles Strozier, *Apocalypse: On the Psychology of Fundamentalism in America* (New York: Beacon Press, 1994).

18. For a discussion of the inherent sexism of the Book of Revelation, see Tina Pippin, *Death and Desire: The Rhetoric of Gender in the Apocalypse of John* (Louisville: Westminster/John Knox Press, 1992). For a discussion of the

homophobic features of apocalypse, see Richard Dellamora, *Apocalyptic Overtures: Sexual Politics and the Sense of an Ending* (New Brunswick: Rutgers University Press, 1994).

19. See Mary Wilson Carpenter's insightful analysis, "Representing Apocalypse: Sexual Politics and the Violence of Revelation," in *Postmodern Apocalypse: Theory and Cultural Practice at the End,* ed. Richard Dellamora (Philadelphia: University of Pennsylvania Press, 1995), p. 110.

20. Robert Jay Lifton, *Thought Reform and the Psychology of Totalism* (1961; Chapel Hill: University of North Carolina Press, 1989), p. 425.

21. Michael Connors, "Hard Times Hit the Promise Keepers," *Time,* 2 March 1998.

22. David Van Biema, "Full of Promise," *Time,* 6 November 1995, pp. 62–63.

23. For discussion of Dobson and Focus on the Family, see *The Religious Right: The Assault on Tolerance and Pluralism in America* (New York: Anti-Defamation League, 1994), pp. 75–84.

24. Minkowitz, "In the Name of the Father," p. 70.

25. Wellington Boone, "Why Men Must Pray," in *Seven Promises of a Promise Keeper* (Colorado Springs: Focus on the Family Publishing, 1994), p. 31.

26. For discussions of American revivalism, see Paul Boyer, *When Time Shall Be No More: Prophecy Belief in Modern American Culture* (Cambridge: Harvard University Press, 1992), chapter 3; Charles Strozier, *Apocalypse: On the Psychology of Fundamentalism in America* (Boston: Beacon Press, 1994), chapter 8; and Robert C. Fuller, *Naming the Antichrist: The History of an American Obsession* (New York: Oxford University Press, 1995), pp. 120–25.

27. Larry B. Stammer, "Teaching Patriarchs to Lead," *Los Angeles Times,* 19 June 1994.

28. Ibid.

29. "Winning the Races," *Christianity Today,* 6 February 1995, p. 23.

30. Bill McCartney, "Seeking God's Favor," in *Seven Promises of a Promise Keeper,* p. 207.

31. McCartney quoted by Randy Phillips in "Seize the Moment," in *Seven Promises of a Promise Keeper,* p. 9.

32. "Christian Men's Movement Taps into Identity Crisis," *Los Angeles Times,* 6 July 1994; p. A10. McCartney's remarks in public have gotten him into some trouble. The ACLU pointed out that he had used the university podium to denounce homosexuality as ungodly and threatened to sue. See Stammer, "Teaching Patriarchs to Lead."

33. "Movement Seeks to Revive Traditional Role for Men," *Washington Post,* 1 August 1994, p. A11.

34. "Manhood's Great Awakening," *Christianity Today,* 6 February 1995, pp. 21–28.

35. Scott Raab, *GQ,* p. 114

36. "New Men for Jesus," *The Economist*, 3 June 1995, pp. 21–22.

37. Laurie Goodstein, "A Marriage Gone Bad Struggles for Redemption," *New York Times*, 29 October 1997, p. A24.

38. Bob Davies, "The Silent Struggle," *Promise Keepers*, September/October 1995, pp. 44–47. Exasperation from reading an article like this prompts me to ponder the kind of question and comment that Adrienne Leban has posed: "Why *exactly* is the Religious Right against homosexuality? It cannot be that the Christian coalitions have risen up just to defend their interpretation that the Bible says homosexuality is sinful. The Bible also forbids greed and hate and killing; but there is no Christian Coalition for National Income Redistribution, or Eagle Forum for Racial Harmony, or Moral Majority for Gun Control." See Adrienne Leban, "Sexual Beggars," *Global City Review*, Sexual Politics Issue, 1 (Spring 1993): 24, 23–28. At the same time, I shudder to think about the political groups that might arise if the Religious Right really did follow to the letter all of the biblical mandates of punishment!

39. Tony Evans, "Spiritual Purity," in *Seven Promises of a Promise Keeper*, p. 73.

40. Gregg Lewis, *The Power of a Promise Kept: Life Stories* (Colorado Springs, CO: Focus On the Family, 1995) p. 108.

41. Evans, "Spiritual Purity," p. 73.

42. June Jordan, "The Case for the Real Majority," in *On Call* (Boston: South End Press, 1985), p. 38.

43. "Winning the Races," *Christianity Today*, February 6, 1995, p. 23.

44. Wellington Boone, "Why Men Must Pray," in *Seven Promises of a Promise Keeper*, p. 31. For an excellent discussion of the apocalyptic implications of actual projects of male pregnancy, see Peter Stokes, "Literature and Apocalypse: Writing, Gender, and the Discourse of Catastrophe," chapter 5, unpublished dissertation, SUNY Stony Brook, 1996.

45. Randy Phillips, "Introduction," *The Power of a Promise Kept*, p. 2.

46. Phillips, *Seven Promises of a Promise Keeper*, p. 9.

47. This phrase, of course, is found in the Catholic church's condemnation of homosexuality and is used by Bill McCartney to explain his position as well. See the premier issue of the Promise Keepers magazine, "The Real McCartney," *New Man*, July/August 1994, p. 36.

6. Feeling Jezebel: Exposing Apocalyptic Gender Panic and Other Con Games

1. Ironically, the astrologer Rob Brezny remarked on this convergence of traditional belief and apocalyptic gullibility in his March 27 column—all but the

mass suicide, of course, since that was happening as his weekly predictions were hitting the stands and Internet. I enjoy checking in with Brezny because of his irreverence:

> This isn't the first time on record that April Fool's Day has fallen in the wake of Easter, but at none of the previous convergences was there also a splashy comet that many conspiracy buffs believe is accompanied by a giant spaceship crammed with aliens. Yup. This is the week the April Fool meets the Resurrected Christ meets the Comet Hale-Bopp in one freaky blow-out bash. What can we expect? A mass conversion of atheist pranksters to Christianity? A new religion –the Hale-Bopp Temple of the Whoopie Cushion?—founded on a recently-discovered gospel which reveals the Lost Jokes of Jesus? Maybe.

Brezny was in fine form that day. If he had known about the Heaven's Gate group death, of course, he might not have been so glib. That horrible incident aside, Brezny deserves to be mentioned as one of the few media folks willing to poke a little fun at a set of beliefs that I personally find at least as bizarre as anything Heaven's Gate came up with. Rob Brezny, "Real Astrology," Internet, 27 March 1997.

2. Michael Kimmel, *Manhood in America* (New York: Free Press 1996).

3. Tina Pippin, "Jezebel Re-vamped," *Semeia* 69–70 (1995): 231.

4. Phyllis Trible, "Exegesis for Storytellers and other Strangers," *Journal of Biblical Literature* 114, no. 1 (1995): p. 4.

5. For full discussion of Jezebel's confrontation with Elijah, see Phyllis Trible, "Exegesis for Storytellers," pp. 3–19; for background to the Yahweh-alone movement, see Norman Cohn, *Cosmos, Chaos, and the World to Come: The Ancient Roots of Apocalyptic Faith* (New Haven: Yale University Press, 1993), chapter 8.

6. Susan R. Garrett, "Jezebel," in *The Women's Bible Commentary*, ed. Carol Newson and Sharon H. Rhinge (Westminster: John Knox Press, 1992), pp. 378–79.

7. Wahneemah Lubiano, "Black Ladies, Welfare Queens, and State Minstrels: Ideological War by Narrative Means," in *Free Spirits: Feminist Philosophers on Culture*, ed. Kate Mehuron and Gary Percesepe (New Jersey: Prentice Hall, 1995), p. 34.

8. Paul Boyer indicates that studies "find evangelism and biblical literalism more pervasive among women, blacks, and older Americans." See his excellent study, *When Time Shall Be No More: Prophecy Belief in Modern American Culture* (Cambridge: Harvard University Press, 1992), p. 15.

9. In this regard, see Tina Pippin, *Death and Desire: The Rhetoric of Gender in the Apocalypse of John* (Louisville: Westminster/John Knox Press, 1992); Mary Wilson Carpenter, "Representing Apocalypse: Sexual Apocalypse and the Vio-

lence of Revelation," in *Postmodern Apocalypse: Theory and Cultural Practice at the End*, ed. Richard Dellamora (Philadelphia: University of Pennsylvania Press, 1995); and Catherine Keller, *Apocalypse Now and Then: A Feminist Guide to the End of the World* (Boston: Beacon Press, 1996).

10. Pippin, *Death and Desire*, pp. 74–75.

11. Result of poll quoted in Daniel Wojcik, *The End of the World as We Know It: Faith, Fatalism, and Apocalypse in America* (New York: New York University Press, 1997), pp. 7–8.

12. Frederick Clarkson, *Eternal Hostility* (Monroe, Maine: Common Courage Press, 1996), chapter 4.

13. "Jezebel, Seducing Goddess of War," Spirit of Life Ministries, Internet, 1997.

14. No name given, "A Prophet's Chamber," Internet 1997. For contact, E-mail address: moonman@rmii.com.

15. Quoted in Patricia Hill Collins, "The Sexual Politics of Black Womanhood," in *Free Spirits*, p. 346.

16. "The Promise Keepettes," *New York Times Sunday Magazine*, 27 April 1997, p. 18.

17. Ellen Fein and Sherrie Schneider, *The Rules: Time-Tested Secrets for Capturing the Heart of Mr. Right* (Warner Books, 1995); Elizabeth Gleick, "Playing Hard to Get," *Time*, 30 September 1996, p. 58.

18. *Millennium*, 24 January 1997, Fox network.

19. James Wolcott, "Too Much Pulp," *The New Yorker*, 1997. Norman Cohn, *Cosmos, Chaos, and the World to Come: The Ancient Roots of Apocalyptic Faith* (New Haven: Yale University Press, 1993), chaps. 12 and 13 in particular.

20. See Susie Bright, *Susie Bright's Sexual State of the Union* (New York: Simon & Schuster, 1996).

Addendum: Circuits of Revelation

1. *Turkey: 1997 Connoisseur's Guide* (New York: Pacha Tour publication, 1997), p. 53.

2. Except for a few revisions, verses 2–6 were written by Betty Bayer and Susan Henking on the occasion of my fiftieth birthday. Thanks!

3. Thanks to Michael Ives for his contribution to my birthday "prophecies." I have quoted from his text and rewritten a few parts.

7. Programmed Perfection, Technoppression, and Cyborg Flesh

1. In a 1993 essay, Katherine Hayles notes that "about 10 percent of the current U.S. population are estimated to be cyborgs in the technical sense, including people with electronic pacemakers, artificial joints, drug implant systems, implanted corneal lenses, and artificial skin. Occupations make a much

higher percentage into metaphoric cyborgs." As I write this in 1997, presumably the figure for both would be higher. See N. Katherine Hayles, "The Life Cycle of Cyborgs: Writing the Posthuman," in *A Question of Identity: Women, Science and Literature*, ed. Marina Benjamin (New Brunswick: Rutgers University Press, 1993), p. 153.

2. In the past decade, of course, Haraway's essay has received both critique and extension (in her own follow-up discussions as well as by others). For both sorts of responses including discussion of numerous other efforts in cultural theory to understand the significance of the cyborg, see Anne Balsamo, *Technologies of the Gendered Body: Reading Cyborg Women* (Durham: Duke University Press, 1996).

3. Donna Haraway, "A Cyborg Manifesto: Science, Technology, and Socialist-Feminism in the Late Twentieth Century," *Socialist Review* 15 (March/April 1985): 67.

4. Also see the critique by Susan Bordo, "Feminism, Postmodernism, and Gender Skepticism," in *Theorizing Feminism*, ed. Anne C. Hermann and Abigail J. Stewart (Boulder: Westview Press, 1994), pp. 458–81.

5. Haraway, "A Cyborg Manifesto," p. 66.

6. It isn't as though Haraway is unaware of this problem. In her "Foreword" to the *Cyborg Handbook*, she strives to make the concept more complex by pluralizing its manifestations to four key post–World War II types. Yet to conclude that essay, she returns to a characterization of "the cyborg" as "a figure for exploring those inventions [of the global and universal], whom they serve, how they can be reconfigured." See Haraway, "Cyborgs and Symbionts: Living Together in the New World Order," in *The Cyborg Handbook*, ed. Chris Hables Gray, with the assistance of Heidi J. Firgueroa-Sarriera and Steven Mentor (New York: Routledge, 1995), pp. xi–xx.

7. Donna Haraway, *Modest_Witness@Second_Millennium.FemaleMan©_Meets_OncoMouse* (New York: Routledge, 1997), p. 271.

8. Paul Virilio, *The Art of the Motor*, trans. Julie Rose (Minneapolis: University of Minnesota Press, 1995), p. 120.

9. Katherine Hayles provides an antidote to that pronouncement by pointing out that the "new cannot be spoken except in relation to the old" and demonstrating how narratives of the posthuman inscribe traditional gender determinants. See Hayles, *The Life Cycle of Cyborgs*, pp. 152–70. Also see Mark Slouka, *War of the Worlds: Cyberspace and the High-Tech Assault on Reality* (New York: Basic Books, 1995) for yet another explicitly antiapocalyptic exploration of technology that turns increasingly apocalyptic as it goes along. Slouka demonizes the techno-scientists themselves as enemies of reality, thus moralizing and mythologizing his position as salvific.

10. Quoted from the video cover. The characterization of the film as "a sexy kinetic thriller" is Graham Fuller's.

11. See Slouka, *War of the Worlds*. As Slouka points out, these efforts are "almost entirely free of political scrutiny" (pp. 69–70).

12. For discussion of the bodily experiences of transsexual surgeries, see Bernice L. Hausman, *Changing Sex: Transsexualism, Technology, and the Idea of Gender* (Durham: Duke University Press, 1995). Hausman provides an important historicization of gender as a concept, demonstrating its emergence in 1955 for a way to describe an intersex child, but readers should be alert to her rather hostile attitude toward transsexual surgery. See chap. 3 in particular.

13. Jean Baudrillard, "The Precession of the Simulacra," in *Simulations*, trans. Paul Foss and Paul Patton (New York: Foreign Agent Series, Semiotext(e), 1983), p. 77, n. 7.

14. Michel Foucault, "On the Genealogy of Ethics," in Herbert Dreyfus and Paul Rabinow, *Michel Foucault: Beyond Structuralism and Hermeneutics* (Chicago: University of Chicago Press, 1983), pp. 237–38.

15. Michel Foucault, *The History of Sexuality*, vol. 1, trans. Robert Hurley (New York: Vintage, 1978).

16. Ibid. p. 1980.

17. In *Anti-Apocalypse* and in an earlier version of this essay, which appeared in *Constellations*, I called the third formation technoppression. After presenting those ideas at a conference on Foucault at Penn State University, I had to rethink the relationship and now I see technoppression as a part of the larger formation of programmed perfection. I am grateful to John Stuhr for bringing the problems of technoppression as I had formulated it to my attention. For the earlier versions, see Lee Quinby, *Anti-Apocalypse: Exercises in Genealogical Criticism* (Minneapolis: University of Minnesota Press, 1994), especially chapter 1, "Eu(jean)ics"; and "Technoppression and the Intricacies of Cyborg Flesh," in *Constellations* (October 1997): 229–47.

18. These estimates were reported on "Prime Time Justice," Court TV, 24 March 1997.

19. For background on racism within such groups, see Michael Barkun, *Religion and the Racist Right: The Origins of the Christian Identity Movement* (Chapel Hill: University of North Carolina Press, 1994).

20. Paul Rabinow is more helpful here. As he has indicated, the "nature" of our lives is increasingly artificial, the product of what he calls "biosociality." Rabinow's extension of Foucault is insightful and guides my thinking about cyber-culture and technoppression. Most pertinent is his insistence that "a multiplication and complex imbrication of rationalities continue to exist. . . .

[O]lder forms of cultural classification of bioidentity such as race, gender, and age have no more disappeared than medicalization and normalization have—although the meanings of and the practices that constitute them are changing." Paul Rabinow, "Artificiality and Enlightenment: From Sociobiology to Biosociality," in *Incorporations*, ed. Jonathan Crary and Sanford Kwinter (New York: Zone, 1992), p. 245.

21. Michel Foucault, "The End of the Monarchy of Sex," in *Foucault Live: Interviews, 1961–1984*, ed. Sylvere Lotringer (New York: Semiotext(e), 1996), p. 223.

22. Michel Foucault, "The Ethic of Care for the Self as a Practice of Freedom," in *The Final Foucault*, ed. James W. Bernauer and David Rasmussen, trans. J. D. Gauthier, S.J. *Philosophy and Social Criticism* 12 (1987), pp. 112–31.

23. Foucault, *History of Sexuality*, vol. 1, p. 106. For further discussion of technoppression and genetics, see Lee Quinby, *Anti-Apocalypse* (Minneapolis: University of Minnesota Press, 1994), chap. 1 on "Eu(jean)ics" and Haraway, *Modest Witness*, chap. 4, "Gene: Maps and Portraits of Life Itself."

24. I owe this use of the term *prosthetics* to Allucquere Rosanne Stone, *The War of Technology and Desire at the Close of the Mechanical Age* (Cambridge: MIT Press, 1996).

25. For the way that psychology as a discipline and practice has been affected by relations with machines, especially in regard to laboratory experimentation, see Betty Bayer, "Between Apparatuses and Apparitions: Phantoms of the Laboratory," in Betty M. Bayer and John Shotter, eds., *Reconstructing the Psychological Subject: Bodies, Technologies, and Practices* (London: Sage Press, 1998).

26. For a fascinating account of both cyberpunk's "redefinition of embodiment," and the response by cultural critics to the cyberpunk movement and this redefinition, see Thomas Foster, "Meat Puppets or Robopaths? Cyberpunk and the Question of Embodiment," *Genders* 18 (Winter 1993): 11–31.

27. Again, these formations of power are heavily imbricated. As I indicated earlier, technological weaponry is integral to alliance's theocratic goals; so is the Internet. Controversy over techno-porn is conducted largely in the rhetoric of the deployments of both alliance and sexuality, with the former advocating V-chip censorship to thwart recruitment into nonnormative sexuality, and the latter enacted in chat room therapy sessions.

28. Foucault proposes problemization by thought as a practice of freedom. Problemization "develops the conditions in which possible responses can be given; it defines the elements that will constitute what the different solutions attempt to respond to. This development of a given into a question, this transformation into a group of obstacles and difficulties into problems

to which the diverse solutions will attempt to produce a response, this is what constitutes the point of problemization and the specific work of thought." Foucault, "Polemics, Politics, and Problemizations: An Interview," in *The Foucault Reader*, ed. Paul Rabinow (New York: Pantheon, 1984), p. 389.

29. R. Dennis Hayes, "Digital Palsy: RSI and Restructuring Capital," in *Resisting the Virtual Life: The Culture and Politics of Information*, ed. James Brook and Iain A. Boal (San Francisco: City Lights, 1995), p. 176.

30. Iain A. Boal, "A Flow of Monsters: Luddism and Virtual Technologies," in *Resisting the Virtual Life*, pp. 11–12.

31. Also see Laura Miller's discussion of the treatment of women on-line, her critique of casting women yet again into the victim role, and her argument against special protections. Laura Miller, "Women and Children First: Gender and the Settling of the Electronic Frontier," in *Resisting the Virtual Life*, pp. 49–57.

32. For discussion of the horror genre as it applies to the Book of Revelation, see Tina Pippin, "Apocalyptic Horror," *Journal for the Fantastic in the Arts* 8, no. 2 (1997): 88–100.

33. Jodi Dean demonstrates the production of paranoia in techno-culture as the nexus of discourses of alien abduction, problems of information flow and blockage, and practices of governmental surveillance. Jodi Dean, *Aliens in America: Conspiracy Cultures from Outerspace to Cyberspace* (Ithaca: Cornell University Press, 1998). I also wish to thank her for both her editorial suggestions and her lively conversations in regard to this paper; ranging as they typically do from cultural theory to extraterrestrial visitors, her insights have been most helpful.

34. In this regard, also see Haraway, *Modest Witness*, chapter 6, "Race: Universal Donors in a Vampire Culture."

WORKS CITED

Aberle, David F. "A Note on Relative Deprivation Theory as Applied to Millenarian and Other Cult Movements." In *Millennial Dreams in Action: Studies in Revolutionary Religious Movements*, edited by Sylvia L. Thrupp. New York: Schocken Books, 1970.

Anderson, Charles. "Thoreau's Monastic Vows." *Études Anglaises* 22 (1969): 11–20.

Armstrong, James. "Thoreau, Chastity, and the Reformers." In *Thoreau's Psychology*, edited by Raymond D. Gozzi. Boston: University Press of America, 1983.

Balsamo, Anne. *Technologies of the Gendered Body: Reading Cyborg Women.* Durham: Duke University Press, 1996.

Barth Fourqurean, Mary Patricia. "Chastity as Shared Strength: An Open Letter to Students." *America*, 6 November 1993, 10.

Baudrillard, Jean. "The Precession of the Simulacra." *Simulations*, translated by Paul Foss and Paul Patton. New York: Foreign Agent Series, Semiotext(e), 1983.

Bayer, Betty. "Between Apparatuses and Apparitions: Phantoms of the Laboratory." *Reconstructing the Psychological Subject: Bodies, Technologies and Practices*, edited by Betty M. Bayer and John Shotter. London: Sage Press, 1998.

Bederman, Gail. "'The Women Have Had Charge of the Church Work Long Enough': The Men and Religion Forward Movement of 1911–1912 and the Masculinization of Middle-Class Protestantism." *American Quarterly* 41 (September 1989): 432–65.

Bercovitch, Sacvan. *The American Jeremiad.* Madison: University of Wisconsin Press, 1975.

Berger, James. *After the End: Representations of Post-Apocalypse.* Minneapolis: University of Minnesota Press, 1999.

Bernstein, Michael Andre. *Foregone Conclusions: Against Apocalyptic History.* Los Angeles: University of California, 1994.

Boal, Iain A. "A Flow of Monsters: Luddism and Virtual Technologies." In *Resisting the Virtual Life: The Culture and Politics of Information*, edited by James Brook and Iain A. Boal, pp. 3–15. San Francisco: City Lights, 1995.

Boone, Wellington. "Why Men Must Pray." In *Seven Promises of a Promise Keeper*, pp. 25–31. Colorado Springs: Focus on the Family Publishing, 1994.

Bordo, Susan. "Feminism, Post-modernism, and Gender Skepticism." In *Theorizing Feminism*, edited by Anne C. Hermann and Abigail J. Stewart, pp. 458–81. Boulder: Westview Press, 1994.

Boyer, Paul. *When Time Shall Be No More: Prophecy Belief in Contemporary American Culture*. Cambridge: Harvard University Press, 1992.

Brezny, Rob. "Real Astrology." [www.realastrology.com], 27 March 1997.

Bridgman, Richard. *Dark Thoreau*. Lincoln: University of Nebraska Press, 1982.

Bright, Susie. *Susie Bright's Sexual State of the Union*. New York: Simon & Schuster, 1997.

Chambers, Veronica. "Young, Hot, and Celibate." *Essence*, July 1993, 56.

"Christian Men's Movement Taps into Identity Crisis." *Los Angeles Times*, 6 July 1994, A10.

Clarkson, Frederick. *Eternal Hostility: The Struggle between Theocracy and Democracy*. Monroe, Maine: Common Courage Press, 1997.

Cohn, Norman. *Cosmos, Chaos, and the World to Come: The Ancient Roots of Apocalyptic Faith*. New Haven: Yale University Press, 1993.

Cohn, Norman. *The Pursuit of the Millennium*. New York: Oxford University Press, 1970.

Collins, Patricia Hill. "The Sexual Politics of Black Womanhood." In *Free Spirits*, edited by Kate Mehuron and Gary Percesepe, pp. 339–51. New Jersey: Prentice Hall, 1995.

Cooper, Marc. "Chastity 101." *Village Voice*, 7 June 1994, 1, 31–5.

Daniels, Ted, ed. *Millennial Prophecy Report*. [http://www.channel.com/mpr].

Davies, Bob. "The Silent Struggle." *New Man*, September/October 1995, pp. 44–47.

Dean, Jodi. "The Truth Is Out There: Aliens and the Fugitivity of Postmodern Truth." *Camera Obscura* forthcoming.

——. *Aliens in America: Conspiracy Cultures from Outerspace to Cyberspace*. Ithaca: Cornell University Press, 1998.

D'Emilio, John, and Estelle B. Freedman. *Intimate Matters: A History of Sexuality in America*. New York: Harper & Row, 1988.

Elmer-Dewitt, Philip. "Making the Case for Abstinence." *Time*, 24 May 1994, 64–65.

Evans, Tony. "Spiritual Purity." In *Seven Promises of a Promise Keeper*. Colorado Springs: Focus on the Family Publishing, 1994.

Fein, Ellen, and Sherrie Schneider. *The Rules: Time-Tested Secrets for Capturing the Heart of Mr. Right*. New York: Warner Books, 1995.

Felman, Jyl Lynn. "Lost Jewish (Male) Souls." *Tikkun* 10 (May/June 1995): 27–30.

Foster, Thomas. "Meat Puppets or Robopaths? Cyberpunk and the Question of Embodiment." *Genders* 18 (Winter 1993): 11–31.

Foucault, Michel. "The End of the Monarchy of Sex." In *Foucault Live: Interviews, 1961–1984*, edited by Sylvere Lotringer, pp. 214–25. New York: Semiotext(e), 1996.

——. "The Return to Morality." In *Foucault Live*, translated by John Johston, edited by Sylvere Lotringer, pp. 465–73. New York: Semiotext(e), 1996.

——. "The Ethic of Care for the Self as a Practice of Freedom." In *The Final Foucault*, edited by James W. Bernauer and David Rasmussen, translated by J. D. Gauthier, S. J. *Philosophy and Social Criticism* 12 (1987): 112–31.

——. *The Use of Pleasure: The History of Sexuality, Volume Two*, translated by Robert Hurley. New York: Pantheon, 1985.

——. "Polemics, Politics, and Problemizations: An Interview." In *The Foucault Reader*, edited by Paul Rabinow, pp. 381–90. New York: Pantheon, 1984.

——. "On the Genealogy of Ethics." In *Michel Foucault: Beyond Structuralism and Hermeneutics*, edited by Herbert Dreyfus and Paul Rabinow. Chicago: University of Chicago Press, 1983.

——. "Two Lectures." In *Power/Knowledge: Selected Interviews and Other Writings, 1972–1977*, edited by Colin Gordon, pp. 78–108. New York: Pantheon, 1980.

——. "Interview with Lucette Finas." In *Michel Foucault, Power, Truth, Strategy*, edited by Meaghan Morris and Paul Patton, translated by Paul Foss and Meaghan Morris, pp. 67–75. Sydney: Feral Publications, 1979.

——. *The History of Sexuality: Volume One: An Introduction*, translated by Robert Hurley. New York: Vintage Books, 1978.

——. "Nietzsche, Genealogy, History." In *Language, Counter-Memory, Practice*, edited by Donald F. Bouchard, pp. 138–64. Ithaca: Cornell University Press, 1977.

Fuller, Robert C. *Naming the Antichrist: The History of an American Obsession*. New York: Oxford University Press, 1995.

Garrett, Susan R. "Jezebel." In *The Women's Bible Commentary*, edited by Carol Newson and Sharon H. Ringe, pp. 378–79. Westminster: John Knox Press, 1992.

Ginzberg, Lori D. "'The Hearts of Your Readers Will Shudder'": Fanny Wright, Infidelity, and American Freethought." *American Quarterly* 46 (June 1994): 195–226.

Giroux, Henry. *Fugitive Cultures: Race, Violence, and Youth*. New York: Routledge, 1996.

Gleick, Elizabeth. "Playing Hard to Get." *Time*, 30 September 1996, 58.

Goodstein, Laurie. "A Marriage Gone Bad Struggles for Redemption." *New York Times*, 29 October 1997, A24.

Gordon, Linda. *Woman's Body, Woman's Right: Birth Control in America.* New York: Penguin, 1977.

Gould, Stephen Jay. *Questioning the Millennium: A Rationalist Guide to a Precisely Arbitrary Countdown.* New York: Harmony Books, 1997.

Graff, Gerald. "Why Theory?" In *Left Politics and the Literary Profession,* edited by Lennard Davis and M. Bella Mirabella, pp. 20–35. New York: Columbia University Press, 1990.

Graham, Sylvester. *A Lecture to Young Men, on Chastity, intended also for the serious consideration of parents and guardians.* Providence: n. p., 1834.

Greven, Phillip. *Spare the Child: The Religious Roots of Punishment and the Psychological Impact of Physical Abuse.* New York: Alfred A. Knopf, 1991.

Hall, Stuart. "Subjects in History: Making Diasporic Identities." In *The House That Race Built: Black Americans, U.S. Terrain,* edited by Wahneema Lubiano, pp. 289–99. New York: Pantheon, 1997.

Haraway, Donna. "A Cyborg Manifesto: Science, Technology, and Socialist-Feminism in the Late Twentieth Century." *Socialist Review* 80 (March/April 1985): 65–108.

Haraway, Donna. *Modest_Witness@Second_Millennium.FemaleMan©_Meets_OncoMouse.* New York: Routledge, 1997.

Harding, Walter. "Thoreau's Sexuality." *Journal of Homosexuality* 21 (1991): 23–45.

Harding, Walter, and Carl Bode. *The Correspondence of Henry David Thoreau.* New York: New York University Press, 1958.

Harding, Walter, and Michael Meyer. *The New Thoreau Handbook.* New York: New York University Press, 1980.

Hatch, Nathan O. "The Origins of Civil Millennialism in America: New England Clergymen, War with France, and the Revolution." *William and Mary Quarterly* 31 (1974): 407–30.

Hausman, Bernice L. *Changing Sex: Transsexualism, Technology, and the Idea of Gender.* Durham: Duke University Press, 1995.

Hayes, R. Dennis. "Digital Palsy: RSI and Restructuring Capital." In *Resisting the Virtual Life: The Culture and Politics of Information,* edited by James Brook and Iain A. Boal, pp. 173–93. San Francisco: City Lights, 1995.

Hayles, N. Katherine. "The Life Cycle of Cyborgs: Writing the Posthuman." In *A Question of Identity: Women, Science and Literature,* edited by Marina Benjamin. New Brunswick: Rutgers University Press, 1993.

hooks, bell. *Teaching to Transgress: Education as the Practice of Freedom.* New York: Routledge, 1994.

"Jezebel, Seducing Goddess of War." Spirit of Life Ministries, Internet, 1997.

Jordan, June. "The Case for the Real Majority." In *On Call,* pp. 37–38. Boston: South End Press, 1985.

Katz, Jonathan Ned. *Gay American History*, rev. ed. New York: Meridian, 1992.

Keller, Catherine. *Apocalypse Now and Then: A Feminist Guide to the End of the World*. Boston: Beacon Press, 1996.

Kimmel, Michael. *Manhood in America*. New York: Free Press, 1996.

Kosofsky Sedgwick, Eve. *Epistemology of the Closet*. Berkeley: University of California Press, 1990.

Kushner, Tony. *Angels in America: Part One: Millennium Approaches*. New York: Theatre Communications Group, 1993.

———. *Angels in America: Part Two: Perestroika*. New York: Theatre Communications Group, 1994.

Lacayo, Richard. "War of Words." *Time*, 7 July 1997, 92.

Landes, Richard. *Relics, Apocalypse, and the Deceits of History*. Cambridge: Harvard University Press, 1995.

Larsen, Elizabeth. "Censoring Sex Information: The Story of *Sassy*." *Utne Reader* July/August 1990, 96–97.

Leban, Adrienne. "Sexual Beggars." *Global City Review*, Sexual Politics Issue, 1 (Spring 1993): 23–28.

Lebeaux, Richard. *Thoreau's Seasons*. Amherst: University of Massachusetts Press, 1984.

Lifton, Robert Jay. *The Protean Self: Human Resilience in an Age of Fragmentation*. New York: Basic Books, 1993.

———. *Thought Reform and the Psychology of Totalism*. 1961. Chapel Hill: University of North Carolina Press, 1989.

Lindsey, Hal. *The Late Great Planet Earth*. Grand Rapids, Mich.: Zondervan, 1970.

Lubiano, Wahneemah. "Black Ladies, Welfare Queens, and State Minstrels: Ideological War by Narrative Means." In *Free Spirits: Feminist Philosophers on Culture*, edited by Kate Mehuron and Gary Percesepe, pp. 34–52. New Jersey: Prentice Hall, 1995.

Magner, Denise. "Ten Years of Defending the Classics and Fighting Political Correctness." *Chronicle of Higher Education*, 12 December 1997, A12–14.

"Manhood's Great Awakening." *Christianity Today*, 6 February 1995, 21–28.

Mason, David. "Mythical Histories." *Hudson Review* (Winter 1993): 659–67.

Matthiessen, F. O. *American Renaissance*. New York: Oxford, 1941.

McCartney, Bill. "Seeking God's Favor." In *Seven Promises of a Promise Keeper*, pp. 205–7. Colorado Springs: Focus on the Family Publishing, 1994.

McClure, Kevin. *The Fortean Times Book of the Millennium*. London: John Brown Publishing, 1996.

McGowan, John. *Postmodernism and Its Critics*. Ithaca: Cornell University Press, 1991.

Millennium. Dir. FOX, 24 January 1997.

Miller, Laura. "Women and Children First: Gender and the Settling of the Electronic Frontier." In *Resisting the Virtual Life: The Culture and Politics of Information*, edited by James Brook and Iain A. Boal, pp. 49–57. San Francisco: City Lights, 1995.

Miller, Nancy K. "Autobiography as Cultural Criticism." In *Getting Personal: Feminist Occasions and Other Autobiographical Acts*, pp. 1–30. New York: Routledge, 1991.

Minkowitz, Donna. "In the Name of the Father." *Ms.*, November/December 1995, pp. 64–71.

Moller, Mary Elkins. "Thoreau, Womankind, and Sexuality." *ESQ* 22 (1976): 123–48.

Morrison, Toni. *Jazz*. New York: Alfred Knopf, 1992.

———. *Playing in the Dark*. Cambridge: Harvard University Press, 1990.

"Movement Seeks to Revive Traditional Role for Men." *Washington Post*, 1 August 1994, A11.

Newman, Judith. "Proud to Be a Virgin." *New York Times*, 19 June 1994, Styles section, 1.

"New Men for Jesus." *Economist*, 3 June 1995, 21–22.

Nissenbaum, Stephen. *Sex, Diet, and Debility in Jacksonian America: Sylvester Graham and Health Reform*. Westport, Conn.: Greenwood Press, 1980.

Nussbaum, Martha. "Feminists and Philosophy." *New York Review of Books*, 20 October 1994, p. 62.

O'Leary, Stephen D. *Arguing the Apocalypse: A Theory of Millennial Rhetoric*. New York: Oxford University Press, 1994.

Peterson, Brian. "God Will Do His Part." Editor's Page, *New Man*, September/October 1995, p. 8.

Phillips, Adam. "Besides Good and Evil." In *On Flirtation*, pp. 59–64. Cambridge: Harvard University Press, 1994.

Phillips, Julia. "You'll Never Get Laid in This Town Again: Why No One's Having Sex in Hollywood." *Gentlemen's Quarterly*, March 1991, pp. 146–7.

Phillips, Randy. "Seize the Moment." In *Seven Promises of a Promise Keeper*, pp. 1–12. Colorado Springs: Focus on the Family Publishing, 1994.

Pippin, Tina. "Apocalyptic Horror." *Journal for the Fantastic in the Arts* 8 (1997): 88–100.

———. *Death and Desire: The Rhetoric of Gender in the Apocalypse of John*. Louisville: John Knox Press, 1992.

———. "Jezabel Re-vamped." *Semeia* 69–70 (1995): 231.

Pudaloff, Ross J. "Thoreau's Composition of the Narrator: From Sexuality to Language." *Bucknell Review* 29 (1985): 121–42.

Quinby, Lee. *Anti-Apocalypse: Exercises in Genealogical Criticism*. Minneapolis: University of Minnesota Press, 1994.

——. "Coercive Purity: The Dangerous Promise of Apocalyptic Masculinity." In *The Year 2000*, edited by Charles S. Strozier and Michael Flynn. New York: New York University Press, 1997.

——. *Freedom, Foucault, and the Subject of America*. Boston: Northeastern University Press, 1991.

——. "'Sex Respect': Thoreau, the Religious Right, and the Problem of Chastity." *Prose Studies* (April 1994): 20–38.

——. "Technoppression and the Intricacies of Cyborg Flesh." *Constellations* (October 1997): 229–47.

Raab, Scott. *GQ*, January 1996, pp. 110–17, 127–30.

Rabinow, Paul. "Artificiality and Enlightenment: From Sociobiology to Biosociality." In *Incorporations*, edited by Jonathan Crary and Sanford Kwinter, pp. 234–52. New York: Zone, 1992.

Rajchman, John. *Michel Foucault: The Freedom of Philosophy*. New York: Columbia University Press, 1985.

Rapping, Elayne. *The Culture of Recovery: Making Sense of the Self-Help Movement in Women's Lives*. Boston: Beacon, 1996.

Richardson, Robert D., Jr. *Henry Thoreau: A Life of the Mind*. Berkeley: University of California Press, 1986.

Rimas, Andrew. "Apocalypse Now?" *The Improper Bostonian* (October 1996): 22–23.

Saliba, Clare. "How the Welfare Bill Could Change the Way Teenagers Learn about Sex." *Village Voice*, 21 January 1997.

Savran, David. "Ambivalence, Utopia, and a Queer Sort of Materialism: How Angels in America Reconstructs the Nation." *Theatre Journal* 47: 207–27.

Schwartz, Hillel. *Century's End*. New York: Doubleday, 1996.

Shamblin, Gwendolyn K. "Weight Loss through Spiritual Gain." *Christian Woman*, May–June 1995, pp. 80–83.

Simpson, Evan, and Mark Williams. "The Ideal of Social Disillusionment." *Philosophical Forum* 26, no. 1 (Fall 1994): 63–77.

Slouka, Mark. *War of the Worlds: Cyberspace and the High-Tech Assault on Reality*. New York: Basic Books, 1995.

Stammer, Larry B. "Teaching Patriarchs to Lead." *Los Angeles Times*, 19 June 1994.

Stearns, Frank P. *Sketches from Concord and Appledore*. New York: n. p., 1895.

Stein, Gertrude. *Ida*. New York: Vintage, 1941.

Stokes, Peter. "Literature and Apocalypse: Writing, Gender, and the Discourse of Catastrophe," Chapter 5. Dissertation SUNY Stony Brook, 1996.

Stone, Allucquere Rosanne. *The War of Technology and Desire at the Close of the Mechanical Age*. Cambridge: MIT Press, 1996.

Strange Days. Director Kathryn Bigelow. Lightstorm Entertainment, 1995.

Strozier, Charles. *Apocalypse: On the Psychology of Fundamentalism in America.* Boston: Beacon, 1994.

Stuhr, John J. "Democracy as a Way of Life." In *Philosophy and the Reconstruction of Culture: Pragmatic Essays after Dewey,* edited by John J. Stuhr, pp. 37–57. Albany: SUNY Press, 1993.

Suddeath, Paula Downey. "How I Broke the Food Chain." *Christian Woman,* May–June 1995, pp. 80–83.

"The Promise Keepettes." *New York Times Sunday Magazine,* 27 April 1997, p. 18.

"The Real McCartney." *New Man,* July/August 1994, p. 36.

The Religious Right: The Assault on Tolerance and Pluralism in America. New York: Anti-Defamation League, 1994.

Thoreau, Henry David. *Early Essays and Miscellanies,* edited by Joseph J. Moldenhauer et al. Princeton: Princeton University Press, 1975.

———. *The Journal of Henry D. Thoreau,* edited by Bradford Torrey and Francis H. Allen. Boston: Houghton Mifflin Company, 1949.

———. *Journal, Volume 2: 1842–1848.* Princeton: Princeton University Press, 1981.

———. *Walden.* Princeton: Princeton University Press, 1973.

Trible, Phyllis. "Exegesis for Storytellers and Other Strangers." *Journal of Biblical Literature* 114, no. 1 (1995): 3–19.

Tuveson, Ernest. *Redeemer Nation: The Idea of America's Millennial Role.* Chicago: University of Chicago Press, 1966.

Van Biema, David. "Full of Promise." *Time,* 6 November 1995, pp. 62–63.

Virilio, Paul. *The Art of the Motor.* Translated by Julie Rose. Minneapolis: University of Minnesota Press, 1995.

Wills, Garry. *Inventing America: Jefferson's Declaration of Independence.* New York: Doubleday, 1978.

Wilson Carpenter, Mary. "Representing Apocalypse: Sexual Apocalypse and the Violence of Revelation." In *Postmodern Apocalypse: Theory and Cultural Practice at the End,* edited by Richard Dellamora, pp. 107–35. Philadelphia: University of Pennsylvania Press, 1995.

"Winning the Races." *Christianity Today,* 6 February 1995, p. 23.

Wojcik, Daniel. *The End of the World as We Know It: Faith, Fatalism, and Apocalypse in America.* New York: New York University Press, 1997.

Wolcott, James. "Too Much Pulp." *New Yorker,* 1997.

Yagoda, Ben. "Retooling Critical Theory: Buddy, Can You Paradigm?" *New York Times,* 4 September 1994, sec. 4, p. 6.

INDEX

UFOs, 20
United States:
   and belief in biblical apoca-
     lypse, 109
   and civil millennialism, 5–6,
     17–18
   and church/state separation, 6
   and global imperialism, 18–19